Extreme Valor

Missouri's Medal Of Honor Recipients

Ross Malone

Copyright: *Extreme Valor: Missouri's Medal of Honor Recipients* Copyright © by Ross Malone. Manufactured in the United States of America. All rights reserved. With excepting the limitations under the copyright reserved above, no part of this publication may be reproduced, stored in or introduced into a retrieval system, or transmitted in any form by any means (mechanical, technological, photocopying, electronic, recording or otherwise), without prior written permission from the copyright owner and the publisher of this book except by a reviewer who may quote brief passages in review.

The scanning, uploading and distribution of this book via the Internet or via any means without the permission of the copyright holder or publisher is illegal and punishable by law. Please purchase only authorized electronic editions and do not participate in or encourage piracy of copyrightable materials. Your support of the author's rights is deeply appreciated.

PUBLISHER'S NOTE: Some of the works in this collection may have been previously published and since modified from initial publication.

To find other books by Ross Malone, order additional print or electronic copies of *Extreme Valor: Missouri's Medal of Honor Recipients* or to contact the author visit:

www.RossMalone.com

or Amazon.com (Ross Malone)

Cover Design and Illustrations by Ross Malone and K. S. Wuertz

First Edition: May 2021

Created and Published in the USA, KSWuertz Publications/Mimosa Lake Press

Library of Congress Cataloging- in- Publication Data

Malone, Ross

Extreme Valor: Missouri's Medal of Honor Recipients/Ross Malone – 1st Edition

ISBN: 9798738088070

"Poor
is the nation
That has no Heros
But poorer still
is the nation
That having heroes,
Fails to remember
and honor them."

Marcus Tullius Cicero

Table of Contents

Show Me More Heroes:

The Medal of Honor

The name of this book is _Extreme Valor_. The words signify that someone is determined, unwavering, or purposeful, high-minded, and courageous. Those words well describe the men and women who have earned the Medal of Honor. Another word that came to my mind for this group of people was intrepid because these people have been so fearless, adventurous, and steadfast in carrying out their duties. Those words very appropriately describe the people we are about to meet.

The Medal of Honor is the highest honor that can be bestowed upon an American man or woman in military service to our country. It is intended to give recognition to an act of extreme valor. In modern times the Medal of Honor is presented by the President of the United States "in the name of Congress." Because of that, it is sometimes incorrectly called the Congressional Medal of Honor.

Each Branch of the Services uses a different version of the Medal. In the illustration, the Army version is shown on the left, the Navy's is in the middle, and the Air Force has a different version which is pictured on the right. The Coast Guard has been authorized to create and present its own version but, so far, they have elected to use the Navy's version. The Marines of course are associated with the Navy so Marines receive the Navy's version of the Medal also. I suppose the new Space Force will need to develop its own version. Several American astronauts have been presented a Space Medal of Honor but it does not have any relationship to the Medal of Honor.

The Medal of Honor grew from a proposal by Lieutenant Edward D. Townsend to his boss, Winfield Scott, the General-in-Chief of the Army in 1861. Surprisingly, Scott squelched the idea saying that it was un-American. He said that medals were a European tradition. But Scott retired and Secretary of the Navy, Gideon Welles picked up the idea and got Congress and President Lincoln to authorize the creation of a medal. The bill was signed into law on December 21, 1861. The first order by the Navy was placed with the U.S. Mint for 175 medals at a cost of $1.85 each.

In the early days, there were vague prerequisites so the medals were relatively easy to come by. In one case 311 men from Maine were given the medal at one time. Their enlistment time had ended so they were bribed to receive a medal if they would just re-up in case there might be another battle in the near future. The unit's records weren't well kept so they just got 864 and passed them out to anyone who might have qualified. In 1916 Congress authorized a group of five retired Generals to review the cases of all medals of honor and insist that they meet the criteria of having to demonstrate "distinguished conduct by an officer or enlisted man in action involving actual conflict with an enemy." The men from Maine lost their medals.

Then, there were the men who received awards for their actions at the Wounded Knee massacre. It's hard to understand how anyone could be rewarded for participating in the murder of mostly old unarmed men, women, and children. Thank goodness none of those people were from Missouri and we didn't have to include them in this book.

Several recipients had their medals revoked because they weren't enlisted in the military when they performed their gallant acts. Those included Buffalo Bill Cody and Mary Edwards Walker, an abolitionist doctor. Buffalo Bill and four other civilian scouts employed by the Army eventually had their medals returned by the Congress of a grateful nation. A few years later, Dr. Walker also received her medal.

Since World War I, a person must "distinguish himself/herself conspicuously by gallantry and intrepidity at the risk of his/her life above and beyond the call of duty." In this book we present every person from Missouri who has ever qualified for the Medal of Honor. We think you will be impressed and possibly inspired.

Medal of Honor Trivia

✪ When a Medal of Honor recipient enters a room, even when he is in civilian clothing, everyone in the room will stand and salute. Even officers of the highest rank will salute a private, airman, or seaman if that person has a Medal of Honor.

✪ Five pairs of brothers have received the Medal of Honor.

✪ General Douglas MacArthur and his father were the first father and son to receive Medals of Honor. The elder Arthur MacArthur won his medal at Missionary Ridge in the Civil War. His son, Douglas won his medal in World War II for his accomplishments in the Philippines.

✪ Only one President has received the honor. That was Theodore Roosevelt for his charge at San Juan Hill. (Spanish-American War) His service was also special because it was ten years after he had served as President.

✪ Teddy's son, Theodore Jr., received a Medal of Honor for valor demonstrated in the Battle at Normandy, World War I

✪ The youngest Medal of Honor recipient was recognized for his actions when he was only eleven years old.

✪ Only nineteen men have earned the Medal of Honor twice.

✪ The first man to receive two Medals of Honor was Thomas Ward Custer, the younger brother of George Armstrong Custer. Those brothers later died together at the Battle of the Little Big Horn.

✪ One Marine asked that his mother's name be engraved on the medal instead of his own. President Nixon complied with the man's wish.

✪ At the Battle of Gettysburg, two Medal of Honor recipients were enlisted as musicians. Among Missouri's recipients, two were musicians.

✪ There are seventy-eight Medal of Honor recipients buried in Missouri Soil.

Extreme Valor:

Missouri's Medal of Honor Recipients

Extreme Valor: Missouri's Medal of Honor Recipients

Ballard, Donald Everett – Vietnam

When you join the Navy, you might be looking forward to adventure. You are likely to anticipate danger in some form. There are all sorts of things creeping into your thoughts but it would probably never cross your mind that you might have hand grenades bouncing off your helmet in some far-away jungle. Welcome to reality for Don Ballard.

Don was born in Kansas City in 1945. By the time he was twenty-years-old, the conflict in Vietnam was turning into a full-fledged war and he chose to jump right in. He asked to be sent to the Navy's Hospital Corps School in Great Lakes. Then he was stationed for a time in Memphis but, by 1968, he was on his way to Vietnam attached to a battalion of Marines. No longer just a Navy medic, he would now be one of the Devil Docs serving the Devil Dogs in the Quang Tri Province. As such, he would not be allowed to fire a weapon except to protect the wounded.

Quang Tri was the northernmost province and just across the border from North Vietnam, so when the Tet Offensive began, Quang Tri was hit hard. On April 29, 1968, 8,000 North Vietnamese infantrymen came across the border and they were backed by heavy artillery. In May, a second phase was launched and over 100 targets were hit simultaneously. It was during this second "Mini-Tet" that Devil Doc Ballard would distinguish himself with his selfless valor.

1

Ballard was with his Company M moving toward the fight when the heat overcame two of the Marines. They collapsed so Ballard saw that they were treated and evacuated by helicopter. Then he caught up with his platoon. At that time, they were ambushed and small arms fire, machine guns, and mortars flew into their position. Ballard jumped into action treating the wounded.

One Marine had especially serious wounds and Ballard directed four other Marines to move him to an area suitable for evacuation. Just as those four arrived, a North Vietnamese soldier jumped up and threw a hand grenade at them. It hit Don Ballard's helmet and fell to the ground right next to the wounded Marine.

Ballard's immediate reaction was to jump on top of the grenade and protect the wounded Marine and the four others. He had a moment to think that grenades are almost always deadly but sometimes the victims survive (with horrible wounds). But, as he thought – and waited – he realized that this particular grenade was a dud. Finally, Ballard stood up, threw the grenade into an empty space, wiped away his sweat and went back to work as if nothing had happened. Then the grenade exploded.

He finished the battle with his unit and finished his tour of duty in Vietnam. He received three Purple Hearts for wounds he received in that war. In 1970 Donald Ballard received the Medal of Honor from President Nixon. When his enlistment with the Navy was up, he enlisted in the Army's Officer Candidate School and earned his commission. When his obligations ended after O.C.S. and his time as an officer, he left the regular Army and joined the National Guard. He retired after thirty-five years of military service in one form or another and after attaining the rank of Colonel.

Don Ballard recently told a reporter from the *Warrensburg Star-Journal*, "My attitude has always been I want to be remembered for what I've done since I came home from combat instead of that one day in combat. The medal is a constant reminder of a lot of guys I didn't save. So I've got the survivor's guilt, my nightmares, and my PTSD at the time was ... about the fact that these guys died in my arms, and crying for their mothers or... It was a terrible experience. I still have trouble with it today."

He spent his final years productively supporting veterans' causes and supporting political candidates who are considerate of veterans and their needs. I think we could all agree that Donald Ballard spent his entire adult life serving the men and women of our military and, by extension, serving all of us in his country.

Barger, Charles Denver – World War I

Charles Barger was one tough guy. But just how tough can we expect anyone to be? He was born in Mt. Vernon,

Missouri to George and Cora Staffelbach. His father was a member of the notorious Staffelbach gang in Kansas and, when Charles was just five years old, his father was convicted and sentenced to time in prison. That's when his mother gave him up for adoption. He didn't see her again for almost twenty years. Fortunately for Charles, he was taken in by Sydney and Phoebe Barger who eventually adopted him. He grew up on their farm at Stotts City, Missouri.

When Charles was twenty-one, he went back to Mt. Vernon and enlisted in the Army. After his Basic Military Training was completed, he was assigned to the Army's 89th Division which was comprised in large part of men from eastern and southeastern Missouri.

His regiment arrived in France in June of 1918 and, within two months, he had been promoted to Corporal and had earned the Expert Rifleman Badge. He was then selected to operate a Chauchat automatic rifle (hand-carried light machine gun) and his ammo man on the gun was another Missourian, Jesse Funk. There will be more about Jesse later in this book.

They fought in the St. Mihiel Offensive and then on to the Meuse-Argonne Offensive. They were pinned down near Bois-de-Banthenville, France with the German Army in the same predicament several hundred yards away. As they sat in this stalemate, the Germans fired high-explosive shells and mustard gas into the Allie's trenches. Night patrols were often sent out to observe the enemy's troop strength, position, armaments, etc. However, on Halloween Day, 1918, the officers in command decided not to wait for the cover of darkness. They sent patrols out during broad daylight.

The Americans were immediately shot down. One officer was shot in both legs and he knew he couldn't run for safety so he ordered his men to leave him there and return to their trenches. As ordered, they left him there in "no man's land" and crawled toward safety. One man did make it back and reported that a 2nd Lieutenant was wounded but still alive. Barger and another man immediately grabbed a stretcher and went out to bring back the wounded officer.

They ran through 500 yards of heavy gunfire and reached the fallen officer. But the officer, Lt. John Millis, had discovered another wounded man was there and he insisted that the other man be taken first. Barger and his assistant took the second man, first Lieutenant Ernest Rowell, to safety and went back into no man's land for Lt. Millis. But Millis had learned of an enlisted man who was still alive and he demanded that the other man be taken away first.

This enlisted man was only 50 yards from a machine gun nest but his rescue was completed and the machine-gunners with the stretcher went into no man's land for a third time to retrieve Lt. Millis. It was because of this incredible bravery that Corporal Charles Barger found himself standing in front of another Missourian, General John J. "Black Jack" Pershing to receive the Medal of Honor.

You will remember that Barger's ammo man was Jesse Funk. After the war, Funk described the Charlie Barger that he knew. "Then there was Charlie Barger. He came from down at Stotts City, Missouri, and he'd never had much of a chance in life. He was an automatic Chauchat gunner; I was his carrier, and I used to write his letters for him and I got to know him pretty well. He was scared, too—just as badly scared as any of us, but he had the grit to put it all behind him, and what was more, he'd force it down so far that he could cheer up the other fellows. Believe me, he sure had grit and I'm proud to have been the running mate of a man that had as much fight in him as he had."

Charles Barger was awarded the Purple Heart for of the times that he was wounded in action! In addition to those Purple Hearts, he also earned the following medals for valor:

- ✪ The Croix al Merito di Guerre (from Italy)
- ✪ The Croix de Guerre (from Belgium)
- ✪ The Medal for Military Bravery (from Montenegro)
- ✪ The Medaille Militaire (from France)
- ✪ The Croix de Guerre with Bronze Palms and Star (from France)
- ✪ The Order of Leopold degree of Knight (from Belgium)
- ✪ The World War I Victory Medal with Three Bronze Stars

- ✪ The Army of Occupation of Germany Medal

- ✪ The Military Medal (from Great Britain)

- ✪ The Medal of Honor

After the war, Charles returned to Missouri and joined an adopted uncle, Henry McFerron, on his farm. He moved on to a construction job in Waco, Missouri but didn't make enough money to get by. He also had problems with blending back into civilian life. Because of these things, Charles enlisted into the Army again at Joplin, 1921. He was sent to Camp Pike, Arkansas where he served until being permanently discharged seven months later.

Charles' life changed there at Camp Pike. While he was there, he met and married Audrey Hurst. A year later, they had a son, Charles, Jr. Sadly, that marriage didn't last but Charles later married Ruth Bailey and they had two children, a boy named Joseph and a girl they called Dodi.

The Kansas City Police Department offered Charles a job in 1922 and the life of a policeman seemed to be a good fit for someone with Charles' military background. Then, after just one month on the job, he and his partner were dispatched to a home where two men were involved in bootlegging and one of them was a suspect in a murder case. The two bootleggers decided to shoot it out with the police.

Barger's partner was shot in the arm and went down. Barger was shot five times, and wounded in one wrist, the other arm, the chest, and the head. Wounded as badly as he was, Charles still managed to shoot both bootleggers.

Barger seemed to recover from his wounds but, in a short time, his head wound, the effects of mustard gas, and his post-traumatic stress disorder seriously affected him physically and mentally. After twelve years with the police department, they released him with no pension or compensation of any kind.

Life was a struggle for Charles after that. Every day was hard. To put food on the table, he raised rabbits and planted a garden. It broke his heart the day that he had to take charity from the American Legion and the V.F.W. but he really had no choice. He told them, "It's fine to have all the medals, but the trouble is you can't eat them."

In 1936 the Great Depression was in full swing and Charles was in his own personal depression as well. He moved to a farm near Oak Grove and started a job with the Civilian Conservation Corps in Blue Springs.

On November 23, 1936, Sheriff's Deputies were dispatched to Charles' home where he was found with a large hunting knife, three self-inflicted wounds to his throat and his house was on fire. His body was badly burned. He lunged at the officers with his knife and the officers fired in self-defense killing Barger. He is buried in the Blue Springs Cemetery in Jackson County, Missouri.

Charles Barger was one tough guy. But just how tough can we expect anyone to be?

Barklely, John Lewis – World War I

John Barkley was born in 1895 and grew up on a farm near Holden. Like many other Missouri farm boys, he considered himself a woodsman and even claimed to be a descendant of Daniel Boone. He certainly was good with a gun but he had problems too.

John had a terrible stammer. Because of his stuttering, he was not accepted when he tried to join the Army. Then the U.S. entered World War I and he tried again but was again turned away. Eventually he was accepted into the Army and his officers realized they had someone they could work with.

At Camp Funston in 1917, they saw a smart and physically fit young man who could hunt, and trap, and he was already a marksman. Someone recognized the skills they needed for intelligence work. He was trained to do reconnaissance missions and report back with the information he had gathered. There in his forward position, he was also valuable as a sniper. They had John in just the right job for him.

John Barkley was near Cunel, France on October 7, 1918. That afternoon he was sent forward to try and locate the German forces. He soon realized that his telephone wire back to camp had been cut and almost immediately he saw German soldiers advancing. Then he also saw an enemy machine gun nest and an abandoned French tank.

The tank's guns had been removed so he grabbed a light

machine gun and as much ammunition as he could carry. Barkley climbed inside that old tank and took cover. Then, for the next two hours he held off several hundred German soldiers. It was just John alone in that old steel shell. All by himself creating a standoff with the enemy until his American comrades realized what was happening and came to his assistance. It was that amazing act that earned him his Medal of Honor as well as five other medals for gallantry from our allies.

Barkley described the action in a letter on display in the National World War I Museum, "I fired my last round of ammunition from the machine gun but kept my automatic pistol for hand to hand fighting [and] plunged out of the tank with a sudden dash. I had three bullet marks on my clothes and a burnt legging string."

After the war, John came back to the farm in Missouri. But the prices for agricultural products had plummeted. John had a hard time trying to support his now-widowed mother and himself. Books about the war were selling very well and he thought he might tell his story and see if the public might want to buy it. He partnered with a writer friend he had met in the war and they produced a book they named *Scarlet Fields*. The publisher forced them to change the name to *No Hard Feelings*. But, while books like *All Quiet on the Western Front* and *Goodbye to All That* were immensely popular, John's book didn't sell well at all.

It could be that the new title wasn't very catchy. It was definitely a factor that his book was released just after the beginning of the Great Depression. Very few people had disposable income for book purchases. The tone of the book certainly went against the sentiments of the time in America. The other books mentioned above were written with strong anti-war messages and that matched the mood of the country in the days following the terrible experience of "the war to end all wars." John's book was about wartime experiences and the value of individual initiative.

Things began to look up for John when he found a job with a detective agency in Kansas City but it wasn't the right job for him. One thing that was right for him was a nice girl from a large dairy farm. John married Marguerite Mullen and her huge quantity of land which they carefully sold to create what is now a suburb of Kansas City. With that, John literally went from rags to riches.

With time, John also found a job that could use his love and knowledge of the outdoors. He became a park supervisor. His goal was to help everyone experience nature the way he had as a boy on that Missouri farm.

The national hero, John Barkley died when he was seventy years old and he is buried in the Forest Hill Cemetery in Kansas City.

Bieger, Charles – Civil War

Charles Bieger was one of the many soldiers who left the unrest in what we now call Germany to a new life in America and found themselves in the American Civil War. He was born (March 25, 1844) in Weisbaden which was in the state of Hesse. He was, therefore a Hessian. Charles was thirteen years old when he came with his family to live where so many Germanic families had settled, in the great valleys of the Mississippi and the Missouri Rivers. Some called the Missouri "The New Rhine."

Specifically, St. Louis was the new home chosen by the Bieger family. When war erupted, Charles joined the 4th Missouri Cavalry and was sent to meet up with another Missouri resident, William T. Sherman's forces in Meridian, Mississippi. Near Okolona, Mississippi Bieger's unit came under fire from rebel forces. Beiger's Captain, Frederick Hunsen, was thrown from his horse and found himself surrounded by the enemy and under heavy gunfire.

Bieger took an extra horse and rode to his Captain's aid. Then he and the officer rode to safety still under a rain of bullets. It was this daring ride that earned the young Private his Medal of Honor.

His Medal of Honor Citation tells us:

"Voluntarily risked his life by taking a horse, under heavy fire, beyond the line of battle for the rescue of his captain, whose horse had been killed in a charge and who was surrounded by the enemy's skirmishers."

Charles Bieger returned to St. Louis after the war. He married and raised three children. He was very gainfully employed as a builder and salesman of travel trunks. Even today, Charles Bieger trunks can be found at auctions and antique sales and are very much prized for their sturdy build and their artistic personalization with lithographs and paint.

Charles died at his St. Louis home when he was eighty-six years old. He is buried in the Mount Hope Cemetery in Lemay, Missouri along with his wife and children. The Medal of Honor Historical Society has recently placed a new commemorative tombstone at his grave.

Addendum:

Possibly the biggest case in the history of the St. Louis Police Department involved two Englishmen. The Victim, Charles Preller, was killed by Hugh Mottram Brooks who was using the name, Walter H. Lennox Maxwell, M.D. The murder came to light when Brooks (Maxwell) left the Southern Hotel and told the desk clerk that his friend, Preller, was traveling but would return soon. He asked that the room be kept and not disturbed.

Soon, the other hotel guests and staff were complaining about a terrible stench coming from that Room 114. When hotel employees entered the room they found several trunks including one that was locked. The police asked a master trunk maker to come to the room and try to open the thing. He did and found a badly decomposed body inside. It was later determined that the man had been killed by chloroform poisoning.

The police began immediately to look for Brooks. They found that he had fled to New Zealand and they immediately filed extradition papers. The entire western world followed the return of the suspect as well as following the colorful trial once he returned. Brooks' mother came from England to make an impassioned plea for "her little chloroformer."

Expert testimony by several people including the trunk maker, who first saw the body and documented what he found, brought Brooks' conviction and execution. I'm sure you've guessed by now that the expert trunk maker who was called by the police was our Medal of Honor winner, Charles Bieger.

Blodgett, Wells Howard – Civil War

Wells Blodgett was born January 29, 1839 in Downers Grove, Illinois. He was one of a family of eight children, seven sons and one daughter. As a young attorney, he worked for a powerful member of the new Republican Party and, this employer served as general counsel for the Rock Island Railroad Company. In one case involving that railroad, a young attorney named Abraham Lincoln was called to help at the office and Wells Blodgett met the future President for the first time. When the Civil War began, Wells immediately enrolled in a unit of Militia. He served that unit as a Private for three months and then joined the National Army with the rank of Lieutenant.

In the autumn of 1862 he marched, with his company and regiment, to Springfield, Missouri, in the army commanded by General John C. Fremont. But as the Confederate Army commanded by General Sterling Price had fallen back to a point farther south, the army commanded by Fremont returned north to a camp near Rolla, that was the western terminus of the Missouri Pacific Railroad.

Sterling Price had withdrawn temporarily from Missouri but in September, 1862 he came back and was moving toward Springfield. Union troops were dispatched from various posts to meet Price's Confederates. On the 30th, Blodgett's unit encountered a large number of Rebels at Newtonia, south of Joplin. They were involved in the First Battle of Newtonia. Blodgett's unit attacked a Confederate garrison but were routed by a superior Confederate force.

General Schofield ordered Blodgett to carry a command to a Union cavalry unit to attack the Rebels. As he and his orderly rode to the cavalry unit, they stumbled on a group of about forty Confederates. Rather than run, the two men attacked and scattered the Rebels. Blodgett and his orderly were able to capture eight enemy soldiers.

It was this action that brought the Medal of Honor to Bloggett. The best description of the events of that day may come from a man who witnessed them.

Brig. Gen. E. B. Brown wrote:

> *"Then General Schofield sent Lt. Blodgett with a single orderly with orders to Col. Hall of the 4th Missouri Cavalry, to move to the left and attack in that direction. The route of the lieutenant was across a piece of woods, in which he suddenly found himself facing a squad of the enemy drawn up in irregular line. Without a moment's hesitation he and the orderly drew their revolvers and charged. The cool impudence of the act nonplussed the foe, and, probably thinking there was a large force in the rear, eight of them threw down their arms and surrendered."*
>
> *It is difficult for me to say which I admired most in the Lieutenant, his bravery in making the charge against such odds when to have hesitated a moment was certain death, or his presence of mind and coolness in offering to accept them as prisioners.*
>
> *"The orderly, too, deserves more than a passing notice. His name is Peter Basnett, and he was at one time Sheriff of Brown County, Wis. The Lieutenant and orderly were well matched—both are quiet and determined men. I am glad to bear witness to the bravery and soldierly conduct of Lt. Wells H. Blodgett, and I hope he will be rewarded as he deserves."*

He had earlier been promoted to Captain and, on New Year's Day, 1863, was commissioned Major and appointed as a Judge Advocate. On November 22, 1864 he was commissioned Colonel and assigned to command the 48th Missouri Volunteer Infantry. On the first of June, 1865, Blodgett was ordered to proceed to Jefferson Barracks in St. Louis with his regiment to be mustered out of the service. Upon its arrival in St. Louis his regiment was said to "present a very fine appearance."

In July 1865, Colonel Blodgett married Emma Dickson and immediately moved to Warrensburg. There he established

a law practice and the voters of that area elected him to serve as their State Representative. Later he was elected to the State Senate. One of his acts in the Legislature was to introduce a bill establishing normal schools at Kirksville and Warrensburg. Of course those are highly respected universities today.

Eventually Wells Blodgett and his family moved to a beautiful home on West Pine in St. Louis and he practiced his legal trade specializing in railroad law. After many happy years in St. Louis, Wells Blodgett died on May 8, 1929 at age 90. He is buried in the Bellefontaine Cemetery at St. Louis.

Burr, Herbert Hoover – World War II

Herbert Hoover Burr was often described with words like "scrappy" or "rough-and-ready." He seems to have been one of those stereotypical G.I.s like we see in the movies. They would drink and brawl at the drop of a hat and they were exactly the men you would want on your side in a fight.

Burr was born on September 13, 1920 in St. Joseph, Missouri.

He had thought about joining the Army but they turned him down, he said because he had bad teeth. So he decided that, if they didn't want him, then he didn't want them either. But when he was twenty-one, the bombs fell on Pearl Harbor and the Army decided they wanted him after all. He told them, "no" but they weren't listening. The draft board soon had him in uniform. Soon after that, he found himself learning to drive tanks across the Mojave Desert.

He took that training to the battlefields of France, Belgium, and then Germany.

In January, 1945 Burr's tank was hit by enemy fire and started to burn. He pulled the driver from the tank and then beat out the flames. All the other crew members were wounded and Burr helped them evacuate and then drove the damaged tank away for repairs.

On March 19, 1945 he was a Staff Sergeant in the 41st Tank Battalion, 11th Armored Division. They were near the town of Dörrmoschel, Germany. He was the gunner in a tank which was hit by an enemy rocket. All of the crew members except Burr bailed out but Burr jumped into the driver's seat and proceeded on into the occupied town.

Just as he entered the town, he encountered a German anti-tank gun. The Germans couldn't know that they were looking at a 24-year-old beer-drinking house painter who was mad at them. The tank's gun didn't work but he was so angry, he didn't need one. Before they could react, he drove directly at their gun destroying it as the crew scattered. After returning to the American line, he ran through hostile fire to bring medical aid to his wounded platoon sergeant. His valor was rewarded with a Medal of Honor.

The Medal of Honor Citation reads:

"He displayed conspicuous gallantry during action when the tank in which he was bow gunner was hit by an enemy rocket, which severely wounded the platoon sergeant and forced the remainder of the crew to abandon the vehicle. Deafened, but otherwise unhurt, S/Sgt. Burr immediately climbed into the driver's seat and continued on the mission of entering the town to reconnoiter road conditions."

The Medal of Honor Citation reads (Cont.):

"As he rounded a turn he encountered an 88-mm. antitank gun at pointblank range. Realizing that he had no crew, no one to man the tank's guns, he heroically chose to disregard his personal safety in a direct charge on the German weapon. At considerable speed he headed straight for the loaded gun, which was fully manned by enemy troops who had only to pull the lanyard to send a shell into his vehicle. So unexpected and daring was his assault that he was able to drive his tank completely over the gun, demolishing it and causing its crew to flee in confusion. He then skillfully sideswiped a large truck, overturned it, and wheeling his lumbering vehicle, returned to his company. When medical personnel who had been summoned to treat the wounded sergeant could not locate him, the valiant soldier ran through a hail of sniper fire to direct them to his stricken comrade. The bold, fearless determination of S/Sgt. Burr, his skill and courageous devotion to duty, resulted in the completion of his mission in the face of seemingly impossible odds."

It was reported that a general once asked Burr how he managed to see that much action and not get wounded.

"Well," Burr answered, "I didn't listen to you guys."

After the war, Burr went back to Kansas City and back to painting houses with his brother. His son, Jack, told the *Kansas City Star* that his dad was always, "a tough, blue-collar guy who worked hard and then went to tip a few after work."

But the tough guy never liked to talk about the war. It wasn't until several years after the incident that his children learned the details of that March 19. Jack told the *Kansas City Star* about the time his father was introduced by Audie Murphy, one of America's most decorated heroes of World War II.

"He said Dad was the first to win the Medal of Honor for careless and reckless driving."

In his later years, his family described him as a gregarious, happy-go-lucky guy who could always come up with a Limerick. They said he was happiest when he was fishing. Herb Burr died on February 8, 1990 in Urbana, Missouri and is buried at Mount Washington Cemetery in Independence.

The Haitian Campaign 1915 –1919

At the turn of the last century Germany used a small community of German settlers to disproportionately wield power in Haiti. In 1914 the United States invoked the Monroe Doctrine to keep European Powers form colonizing the Americas. The U.S. seized the Haitian National Bank and stabilized the debt-ridden economy. With the more stable economy, Haiti was able to begin repaying its European debtors.

In 1915 the Haitian President executed 167 political prisoners and sparked an uprising. He was lynched and the country rioted. The United States sent the USS Washington into the Harbor at Port-au-Prince and the Marines took control of the capital city. Within days the Marines established martial law and censored the press. In a short time, a new government was in place with a new constitution and the situation began to improve.

The Marines brought stability and progress. In a short time, 1,700 miles of roads had been built, 189 bridges were built, and irrigation canals were rebuilt. Many hospitals, schools, and public buildings were constructed and clean drinking water was brought to the cities. The increased prosperity allowed the government to repay most of its debts.

But there were still problems. Many Haitians, especially in rural areas, resented the presence and dominance of any foreign power, even American. An armed opposition group called the Cacos emerged under the leadership of Charlemagne Péralte. American diplomats labeled Péralte "the supreme bandit of Haiti." They decided that he must be arrested or killed.

A detachment of Haitian Gendarmerie under the leadership of St. Louis Marines, Corporal William Button and Sergeant Herman Hanneken was sent to subdue the rebel leader. They disguised themselves as peasants and passed quietly through the countryside always moving toward the reported location of the Cacos. As they got closer, they learned that most of the rebels would be away that night attacking a small town and looting it for supplies. There were still six camps of Péralte's guards who were stationed around him for protection. Button and Hanneken were able to elude the soldiers in four camps but were finally discovered.

They fought their way into the final camp and located Péralte. He refused to be arrested and his men would not let the arrest take place and the fighting continued. Finally Button fired a shot through Péralte's heart and they put his body across the back of a mule and took him to Port-au-Prince. That night about 1,200 rebels were killed, captured or dispersed.

Then the diplomats made a very undiplomatic decision. They decided to make an example of Péralte and show the people what happens to rebels. They tied his body to a door and took a photo to be distributed throughout the nation. But the plan backfired. The people saw the image as resembling a crucified Christ and Péralte became a martyr stirring a larger rebellion in which 3,250 Haitians died.

The U.S. occupation of Haiti ended in 1935 and we remain two friendly nations but Charlemagne Péralte is revered as one of their greatest national heroes.

Button, William R.

The Haitian Campaign

Will Button was born December 3, 1895 in St. Louis. He was the youngest of three children and the only boy. He joined the Marines in 1917 and was sent to Haiti in 1919. One could argue that the diplomats blundered their handling of the death of Charlemagne Péralte but no one could criticize the way that Will Button or Henry Hanneken carried out their orders. They completed their most difficult mission with precision and focus. **Button's Medal of Honor Citation reads as follows:**

"For extraordinary heroism and conspicuous gallantry
and intrepidity in actual conflict with the enemy
near Grande Riviere, Republic of Haiti,
on the night of October 31 - November 1, 1919,
resulting in the death of Charlemagne Péralte,
the Supreme bandit chief in the Republic of Haiti,
and the killing and capture
and dispersal of about twelve hundred (1200)
of his outlaw followers.

Corporal William R. Button
not only distinguished himself by his excellent
judgment and leadership, but unhesitatingly exposed
himself to great personal danger, when the slightest
error would have forfeited not only his life
but the lives of the detachments of Gendarmerie
under his command,

The successful termination of his mission will
undoubtedly prove of untold value to
the Republic of Haiti."

After Button's Medal of Honor ceremony, he took a short furlough and returned to visit his family in St. Louis and then returned to Haiti, this time as a Sergeant. He died of malaria on April 15, 1921 at the Department Hospital in Cap-Haïtien, Haiti. He was only twenty-five years old. He is buried in the Valhalla Cemetery in South St. Louis County.

Today our Navy and Marines are supplied with the cargo brought to them by a container ship, the USNS Button, named in honor of this hero of Haiti.

Hanneken, Herman Henry

Herman Hanneken was born in St. Louis on June 23, 1893. He was twenty-one when he enlisted in the Marines. He rose through the enlisted ranks and, within five years, he held the rank of Sergeant.

He served in the Banana Wars of Central America and then was sent to Haiti. There you know that he put an end to the rebel leader, Charlemagne Péralte, for which he received the Medal of Honor. In the uprising that followed Péralte's death, another rebel leader arose and Hanneken killed him. For his bravery in that action, he received the Navy Cross. In Nicaragua he received another Navy Cross.

He was stationed stateside for over ten years but was called to duty in the Pacific during World War II. In that Pacific Theater he received the Silver Star, the Legion of Merit, and the Bronze Star. In 1948, he retired after thirty-four years of service and at the rank of Brigadier General.

Herman Hanneken the highly-decorated hero who rose from Buck Private to Brigadier General died on August 23, 1986 at age ninety-three.

Cary, Robert Webster, Jr. – Interim

Robert Cary was born in Kansas City on August 18, 1890. He was the son of Robert Cary and Lalla Marmaduke Cary. His father and grandfather were judges of the Jackson County Court and the elder Cary was one of the men responsible for building the brick courthouse at Independence. His mother was the daughter of one Missouri Governor and the niece of another. In fact, his parents had been married in the Governor's Mansion.

Robert Jr. was an only child and not much is known about childhood but, after graduation from high school in 1908, he began leaving a trail of excellence. He went first to the University of Missouri. But then, during his third semester, he learned that he had been accepted into the Naval Academy at Annapolis. He was a freshman at Annapolis when his father died unexpectedly in Kansas City.

At the Naval Academy he was known as "Bob" and sometimes as "Skipper" because he was the Captain of the Reina Mercedes, a captured ship which was used as a barracks at the Naval Academy. He was on the track team all four years as well as the wrestling, swimming, and gymnastics teams. He also served as Manager of the track team.

In the Academy's yearbook, "The Lucky Bag," Midshipman Cary was described as follows:

> *"Barring none, I would say that Bob is the man in our class who can with the least exertion get the most results. He, though an expert grafter, is efficient for the reason that he knows how and what to do. In scholarship he may not stand one. Knowing the bearing of the Battle of Lissa to the present civilization or the relation between the theory of the rigidity of the trajectory in vacuum and that in air is a small matter. Bob doesn't know these and, furthermore, doesn't care to know them. He does know how to handle men as evidenced by his superb work as "ratey" three-striper plebe summer. The Commandant congratulated him most heartily on his leadership by a trip to Philadelphia. Bob knows the common sense thing to do under all circumstances and does it."*

> *"As a business man "Skipper" Cary has few equals. He runs things in a clean, systematic manner; he works all the time to carry out his plans; when he tells you that he is going to do a thing, he does it. As Assistant Manager Second Class year of the Wrestling, Swimming, Gymnasium and Track teams he managed them all by himself, because the 1st Class Manager was in love and unsatisfactory in Electricity. His work was without criticism."*

> *"This book would not be one-half what it is if Skipper hadn't gone into his work with the interest, zeal and energy characteristic solely of Skipper. He was manager of the Photographic Department, and he*

> *managed it, too. No picture was too hard for him to get; no trouble was too hard for him to bear. "Skip," we owe much, yes, very much of it to you."*

> *"But there are two sides to every question. Though a stern business man, the Skipper, a veteran dyed-in-the-wool fusser, is one of the best fellows on earth. Philadelphia, Washington, New York, yea, even Kansas City will vouch for this. Make a liberty with him and then you will swear that there is none better. He has a certain knack of having a good time; and being blessed with experience along this line, he is able to get a good time out of anything and give you the larger part of it."*

Immediately after graduation, Cary was granted a short period of leave during which time he was invited to speak at the Bonaventure Hotel in Kansas City. The subject of his talk was "To Do a Thing Right and Well." He graduated from the Academy with the class of 1914. Within just a few months, he earned the Medal of Honor. This leave of absence was partially the result of his first ship, the USS Stocton being still in the final stages of construction.

It was January 21, 1915 when the young Ensign Cary was observing the firerooms of the USS San Diego. He had just started to record his hourly readings of the steam pressure at every boiler. He finished Fireroom No. 2 and was stepping through the electric watertight door into Fireroom No. 1 when the boilers behind him exploded.

As the doors were being closed by controls on the Bridge, Ens. Cary held the doors open and yelled for the men in No. 2 Fireroom to escape. Three of them did. He had to stand for probably a minute in the escaping steam in order for the men to get out. His coolness under pressure helped to keep the other men at other boilers at their posts as they killed the fire under every boiler.

Five boilers in their immediate vicinity exploded that day and two others were likely to explode at any second. But the men stayed at their positions and shut the boilers down.

When the fires under the boilers had been doused, Ens. Cary directed the men into the bunker. They all understood the danger of the final two boilers exploding. During the entire time Ens. Cary was calm and collected and showed an abundance of nerve under the most trying circumstances. The ship's staff decided that Cary's actions were above and beyond the call of duty. They recommended him for the Medal of Honor.

It was an amazing beginning to a most illustrious career. He served for over thirty years and through two World Wars. One ship that he was commanding was struck by a radio-controlled German glide bomb. On another occasion, a hurricane blew a depth charge loose and it dangled off the fantail of the USS Sampson threatening to swing into the ship and explode. Cary and three enlisted men went to the fantail and secured the depth charge while in great danger of being swept overboard themselves. It's no wonder that Kansas City's Robert Cary became one of the most decorated officers in the history of the United States Navy.

He was awarded many honors over the years including the Navy Cross, the Legion of Merit, the Distinguished Service Order (UK), and our nation's highest honor, the Medal of Honor.

Rear Admiral Cary died July 15, 1967 and is buried in the Arlington National Cemetery.

Cole, Darrell Samuel – World War II

There used to be a little town in Missouri's Mineral Area called Esther. Darrell Samuel Cole was born there on July 20, 1920. Years later Esther merged with Flat River, Elvins, Rivermines, and the former village of Fairview Acres to form the present city of Park Hills.

Darrell attended school and the Esther Baptist Church in Esther where people often called him "Coley." In high school he was active in basketball, hunting, photography, and the school music program where he learned to play the French horn. He graduated during the Great Depression and couldn't find a job so he joined the Civilian Conservation Corps. Four months before Pearl Harbor he joined the Marine Corps.

He asked for duty as a machine gunner but they saw that he played the French horn so they made him a company bugler. There was a shortage of buglers. After completing field music school, he was transferred to a combat unit. His repeated protests and requests did no good and he continued to be the company bugler even as they were shipped into combat.

On his second overseas tour of duty, he was taking part in the Battle of Guadalcanal and on August 7, 1942, the Marines found themselves in need of more machine gunners so Darrell Cole got to fill in. After Guadalcanal, Darrell fought in the Battles of Kwajalein, Saipan and Tinian and, beginning with Saipan, Darrell carried a machine gun instead of a bugle.

During the fighting on Saipan, his squad leader was killed and Cole assumed command of the entire squad even though he was wounded. He was awarded the Purple Heart and the Bronze Star for "...his resolute leadership, indomitable fighting spirit and tenacious determination in the face of terrific opposition."

At Tinian in the Marianas, Cole led his squad ashore and continued to build a reputation for himself as "The Fighting Field Musician." By November, Cole had been promoted to the rank of Sergeant.

February 19, 1945 found Cole and his machine gun squad landing on Iwo Jima. The island was a key to victory because its airfields were close enough to allow our bombers and escort planes to reach the Japanese mainland. The fighting to defend that island and its airbases was horrific. As Coles gunners advanced, they found themselves caught in the crossfire of two machine gun emplacements and they couldn't move forward or back. They were pinned down. Sergeant Cole personally destroyed those two emplacements with hand grenades.

As they moved forward once again, they found themselves pinned down for a second time. This time three machine gun emplacements had them in their sights. Cole's machine gun jammed so he made a one-man attack against the three enemy positions armed only with his hand gun and one grenade. Twice he braved fierce enemy fire to return to his squad for more hand grenades. Finally he destroyed the third and final Japanese machine gun.

Cole returned to the safety of his own squad's location when a hand grenade landed nearby and he was killed. But, of course, his squad was able to move forward and be a part of the great victory.

At the request of his father, Darrell Cole's remains have been brought home and he is buried at the Parkview Cemetery in Farmington, Missouri.

Footnote:

To honor this Marine hero of Iwo Jima, the Navy named a new destroyer for him. The USS Cole is an Aegis-equipped guided missile destroyer. Some will remember that, on October 12, 2000, the Cole was anchored at the port of Aden in Yemen. She was damaged that day in a suicide bomb attack. She was quickly repaired and serves from her base in Virginia.

Crandall,
Orson Leon –
Interim

Orson Crandall was one of the very few who earned his Medal of Honor during peacetime. Some will disagree with the correctness of his recognition because of that. But let's look at what he did and you decide whether he deserves such a high honor or not.

Orson was one of several Medal of Honor recipients who was born in St. Joseph. Born February 2, 1903, he was the

youngest of four children of Marshall and Bertie (Bennett) Crandall. He doesn't seem to have been any sort of standout in his school or community but when he reached the Navy, all that changed. He worked his way up from the basic boot to eventually receive a Commission as Lieutenant.

While a Chief Boatswain's Mate, he took the courses offered by the Navy and became a diver. Eventually he was a

Master Diver and that is how he came to be called on for his expertise, skill, and courage on May, 23, 1939. That is the day when a United States Submarine sank with all hands on board.

Chief Crandall was aboard the USS Falcon (ASR-2) when she was called to try and rescue the submariners trapped in the sunken USS Squallus. She was a newly-commissioned diesel electric submarine on a test run. She completed eighteen dives but, on the nineteenth, suffered a catastrophic valve failure and sank off the Isle of Shoals

Arriving at the coordinates of the accident, the five divers involved learned that twenty-six of the crew had died but more than thirty were still alive 240 feet down and praying for someone to figure out a way to rescue them. Chief Crandall and four other divers responded. They were knowledgeable about the use of the newly-developed McCann rescue chamber. That was a revised version of a diving bell. So, over the next 13 hours, all thirty-two crewmen and one civilian expert were rescued from the partially flooded submarine.

Then, on 13 September, after Chief Crandall and the other divers led a long and difficult salvage operation, the new multi-million-dollar submarine was raised and towed into the Portsmouth Navy Yard. The boat was formally decommissioned on 15 November, renamed Sailfish on 9 February 1940, and recommissioned on 15 May 1940 in time to see a great deal of action in World War II. She won nine Battle Stars in the Pacific Theater. Chief Crandall also saw a great deal of action in that conflict.

Lieutenant Crandall was a career Navy man from the middle of the continent who finally, after thirty years, retired with his wife, Mary, to a home near the sea at St. Petersburg, FL. He died there in May 10, 1960 at the age of fifty-seven.

In addition to the Medal of Honor, this highly skilled and courageous veteran had another posthumous honor. In 1967, the U.S. Navy commissioned YHLC-2, a salvage lifting craft, as the USS Crandall. He would have been so pleased!

David, Albert Leroy – World War II

Remember the old movies about adventure on the high seas? Do you remember how one ship might capture another? Buccaneers did it all the time! Seizing an enemy's ship used to be considered quite a prize. But the last time that happened was way back in the War of 1812. Until. . .

Albert Leroy David was born on 18 July 1902 in Maryville, Missouri and grew up there as the son of the Nodaway County farm couple.

Shortly after his seventeenth birthday he enlisted in the Navy. He completed Boot Camp and then served aboard a succession of Battleships and Cruisers. He reenlisted in May, 1931 and was assigned to a Destroyer Tender, the USS Dobbin, and remained on board until August 1939, when he was placed in the Fleet Reserve. In the very next month, the war began in Europe and he was called back to active duty. He received a temporary promotion to the Warrant Officer rank of Machinist and was ordered to the Submarine Repair facilities in San Diego.

In June of 1942 Albert made the jump to Ensign and was sent to diesel engineers' training. Eventually, he was sent to Orange, Texas to help fit-out and serve aboard a Destroyer Escort, the USS Pillsbury. In May 1943, he received another temporary promotion. This time to Lieutenant Junior Grade.

June 4, 1944 was a fateful day for LTJG David. His ship, the USS Pillsbury, was a part of the USS Guadalcanal's task force which was escorting convoys off the coast of French West Africa. A German U-Boat, the U-505, spotted the convoy but the task force spotted the submarine, damaged it badly, and forced it to surface.

David led a nine-man team on board the submarine and took possession of it. He took the crew as prisoners and, even though the boat was flooding and in danger of exploding, they located the code books and other important materials. Then he directed the initial salvage operations to make certain that the submarine was seaworthy and it was towed to a friendly port in Bermuda and her crew was sent to a POW camp. Possibly the main significance of the event was the capture of the code books, charts, enigma coding machines, and other information about U-Boat operations. These materials also allowed the Allies to decode German submarine radio messages in real time, which led to greater successes in the European theater.

The U-505 sits today inside the Museum of Science and Industry in Chicago and many of this book's readers have probably toured the claustrophobic nightmare. But, if you should go again, be sure to look for the Lieutenant David's Medal of Honor. It's on display there with the captured sub.

The next month, David was promoted to Lieutenant and found that he was to receive the Medal of Honor. But less than a month before he could receive the medal, he died of a heart attack. (September 17, 1945) His widow, Lynda (Betts) David was called to the White House to receive his medal from the President Truman.

Lieutenant David received many honors over the years but one that he may have appreciated the most came when the Navy commissioned a new Destroyer Escort in his name, the USS Albert David.

Davis, Freeman – Civil War

Try to imagine the scene as Freeman Davis sat on his front porch and a special package was delivered to him. Picture his surprise as he realizes it is from the President of the United States.

A history book from Bates County, Missouri tells us about that moment.

"Some years later, on March 30, 1898, the corporal received a telegram. Sitting on the porch of his home at 410 Delaware in Butler, Missouri, he attached his glasses and began to read. Just another government form letter? Not this time..."

"The President of the United States on behalf of the congress and a grateful nation is pleased to inform you that you have been awarded the medal of honor for your heroic actions at the Battle of Missionary Ridge, Tennessee, on November 25, 1863."

The corporal was now 56 years of age, in failing health and in fact would be gone in less than a year. ...."

A local newspaper also described that event.

Last week Captain Freeman Davis, of our city, received from the War Department, a Medal of Honor for gallantry at the battle of Missionary Ridge, November 25, 1863. It was enclosed in a satin lined case, is made of bronze in the shape of

a star and the design and workmanship beautiful. It was accompanied by an autograph letter from Secretary of War, Alger, stating that it was awarded Capt. Davis by an act of Congress. On the back is engraven the following: The Congress to Captain Freeman Davis, 80th Ohio Infantry, for gallantry at Missionary Ridge, Tenn. Nov. 25, 1863."

Just for clarity, in his later years, Davis was a Captain in the Grand Army of the Republic, a veterans group. But he was not an officer in the war.

Let's go back a few years and learn a little more about this quiet man. Freeman was born on the last day of February, 1842 in Newcomerstown, Tuscarawas County, Ohio. He was eighteen when the Civil War erupted and he joined up with the 80th Ohio Infantry. Two years later he would become famous at the Battle of Missionary Ridge in Tennessee.

To really understand the significance of Freeman Davis' act is probably hard to do with our modern mindset and our current understanding of how battles are successfully waged. The Civil War was a turning point for such things. In prior wars, lines of brightly clad armed men marched toward each other until their officers ordered them to engage the enemy with shot or a charge. There was a good deal of polished brass, flags billowing, drums and bugles. A part of the "shock and awe" of that day was the impression that a well-uniformed and fully-assembled army presented to intimidate its foe.

Each unit marched under its own unique battle flag and followed that flag into combat. The flag was never to falter or fall. The capture of an enemy flag was seen as something worthy of a great deal of pride. To let the flag fall into the hands of the enemy would be a disgrace.

It was November 25, 1863 and a battle was raging in a place called Missionary Ridge in Tennessee. The Union forces were not doing well and were being forced to fall back. As he retreated with his unit, Sergeant Davis looked around to see the two men who carried Union flags had been shot and were down. Going back through that heavy fire, Davis grabbed one flag in each hand and brought them back. This kept them from being captured by the Confederates.

After the War Freeman Davis settled into a quiet life in Butler, Missouri. It may be that his wife was from Butler but no one seems to know just why they chose that small community on the short grass prairie of Missouri.

They seemed to have lived a typical life and raised four children in their home on Mill Street. Freeman was employed at the local woolen mill. Freeman's wife, Annie's health declined in her later years and she died on December 11, 1886. She was buried in the Oak Hill Cemetery.

Freeman followed his wife on February 23, 1899 and was buried in the Oak Hill Cemetery with full military honors.

Thanks:

Our thanks to Peggy Buhr, Museum Director, at the Bates County Historical Society & Museum. Freeman Davis' story would not be complete without her assistance

Trivia:

The first Rebel flag captured by a Union force in the entire Civil War was on May 15, 1861. Nathaniel Lyon's Fifth Missouri Volunteers were in DeSoto, Missouri because of a reported secessionist meeting. At the meeting, a "large states' rights flag" was planned to be raised. They found it and seized it. This was the first rebel flag taken during the Civil War. But there's more to the story. The troops could not, at first, find the flag because it had been hidden. Finally, they found it under the dress of a woman who was in bed pretending to be sick. They made her stand up and the flag fell out. Such was the glory of capturing that first enemy flag.

Ellis, Michael B. – World War I

Anthony and Ann Krzyzanowski Eliasz came to America from Poland in 1879. They made their home in St. Louis and that's where, on October 28, 1894, their son Michael was born. Michael's mother died while he was still an infant and his father didn't feel that he could care for the baby properly so he gave him up for adoption. A Polish family, the Mocsdlowskis, lived across the river in East St. Louis and they took the baby in.

We know that he attended the St. Laurence O'Toole parochial school but not much more about his childhood. When he was twelve, Michael quit school and went to work in his father's print shop. He was eighteen when he went to Jefferson Barracks and enlisted in the Army. At this time, he was using the anglicized last name, Ellis.

His infantry unit served along the Mexican border and then, in 1914, he served at the occupation of Veracruz. When his three-year enlistment was up, he received an honorable discharge and returned to civilian life. After just six months of that, he re-enlisted.

When the U.S. entered World War I, Michael was sent to France and saw action at Soissons and was awarded the Silver Star. He was promoted to Corporal in April of 1917 and to Sergeant just one month later. The official record of the War Department tells us:

"He showed unusual courage in carrying supplies and in attacking strong points at Brouil, Pleissy, and Berney-le-Sac. Our allies, recognizing Sergeant Ellis' bravery, awarded him the Chevalier Legion of Honor of France, and the Croix de Guerre with Palm, the Cross of War from Italy, Cross of War of Poland, and Recognition by the Moroccan Government with two medals, Senior and Junior.

That Cross of War from Poland was especially significant because the stocky little 5' 5" Ellis was becoming a celebrity and source of pride for Polish-Americans in uniform and back at home. In the nation's newspapers he was being celebrated with nicknames like Machine Gun Mike, the Lone Wolf, and, eventually, the Sergeant York of St. Louis.

On October 5, 1918, Ellis was a part of the Hundred Days Offensive near Exermont in northeastern France. He moved ahead of his company and single-handedly attacked several machine gun nests. In total, he silenced eleven machine guns and captured dozens of enemy soldiers. After many skirmishes throughout France, he was promoted to First Sergeant.

In August 1919, he returned to St. Louis, where another Missourian, General John J. Pershing, presented him with the Medal of Honor for his actions near Exermont. He was the only soldier in Pershing's 1st Division to receive this award. His Medal Citation details what he did to deserve his nation's highest honor:

"The President of the United States of America, in the name of Congress, takes pleasure in presenting the Medal of Honor to Sergeant Michael B. Ellis (ASN: 56976), United States Army, for extraordinary heroism on 5 October 1918, while serving with Company C, 28th Infantry, 1st Division, in action at Exermont, France. During the entire day's engagement Sergeant Ellis operated far in advance of the first wave of his company, voluntarily undertaking most dangerous missions and single-handedly attacking and reducing machinegun nests. Flanking one emplacement, he killed two of the enemy with rifle fire and captured 17 others. Later he single-handedly advanced under heavy fire and captured 27 prisoners, including two officers and six machineguns, which had been holding up the advance of the company. The captured officers indicated the locations of four other machineguns, and he in turn captured these, together with their crews, at all times showing marked heroism and fearlessness."

The war ended and Mike returned to St. Louis for discharge as the most highly decorated Polish-American in World War I. This time he permanently returned to civilian life. On January 2, 1921, Ellis met an old childhood playmate, a young woman of Polish descent. They were married two years later, in St. Louis.

He received a wonderful honor after the war when President Theodore Roosevelt wrote about him in a series of newspaper articles entitled, "America's Heroes of the Great War."

Despite being such a hero, Mike had trouble finding a job. His aim was to find steady employment with the US Post Office but he always seemed to have trouble with their competitive Civil Service exams. Eventually, President Calvin Coolidge intervened and ordered the Post Office to waive Mike's exam and put him to work.

Life was better from that point onward but it was just too short. On December 9, 1937, Michael (Eliasz) Ellis succumbed to pneumonia and died at age forty-three. He was buried with full military honors at the Arlington National Cemetery.

Falconer, John A. – Civil War

John Falconer's life began on New Year's Day, 1844 in Washtenaw County, Michigan. The 1860 Census shows that he was living with his parents, Peter and Grace Falconer who had emigrated from Scotland more than twenty years earlier, along with John's grandparents. Peter was a farmer and John had quit school by that time to work on the family farm. Little else is known about him until he enlisted in the 17th Michigan infantry for duties in the War Between the States on June 21, 1862. He was eighteen-years-old at that time.

In November of 1863 his unit was involved in the Battle for Knoxville and specifically with defending Fort Sanders. The Confederate forces had tried unsuccessfully to storm the fort but had fallen back. Then they set about emplacing cannon and mortar to shell the fortress in preparation for another attack. In addition, they had one farmhouse which they filled with observers and snipers to harass the Union defenders. The snipers proved to be very deadly. Brigadier General Ferrero said they were, "doing material damage to my line of skirmishers."

It was then that John Falconer and four other men formed what they called "the burning party." While men form Fort Sanders gave a covering fire this small group of men rushed for approximately 1,000 yards through Confederate fire and sniper fire from the house to set the house ablaze and force its occupants out. All but Falconer and one other volunteer were killed in that action. When the Union troops finally rushed from the fort to engage the Rebels, the way was much easier because there was no advanced warning and no sniper fire from the house. It was for his valor on this day that John Falconer was granted a Medal of Honor. His Medal Citation read:

"The President of the United States of America, in the name of Congress, takes pleasure in presenting the Medal of Honor to Corporal John A. Falconer, United States Army, for extraordinary heroism on 20 November 1863, while serving with Company A, 17th Michigan Infantry, in action at Fort Sanders, Knoxville, Tennessee. Corporal Falconer conducted the "burning party" of his regiment at the time a charge was made on the enemy's picket line, and burned the house which had sheltered the enemy's sharpshooters, thus ensuring success to a hazardous enterprise."

After the War, John met and married Eliza Puckette whose parents had moved from Kentucky to Knob Noster, Missouri. John and Eliza decided to stay nearby so he lived the rest of his life in Warrensburg. Their home was at 416 West

Fourth Street. They seem to have had only one child, Grace. John died on April 1, 1900 and he is buried at the Sunset Hill Cemetery in Warrensburg. Eliza remarried and moved west to Colorado.

Almost a hundred years passed and John's old standard military tombstone was worn and in bad shape. So the folks in Warrensburg decided to do something about it. They were somewhat surprised to learn that only family members can request a new grave marker and no family members could be found. Then in December of 1998, Betty Harvey Williams, with the Johnson County Missouri Historical Society, discovered a letter from 1958 filed away and forgotten. In the letter, Grace Ackerly identifies herself saying, "I am the sole survivor of John Falconer." With this, it was possible to request a new stone – and this one indicated John's Medal of Honor status.

On June 12, 1999, a special ceremony was organized by the Medal of Honor Society, Johnson County Missouri Historical Society, and the Sons of Union Veterans of the Civil War 1861-1865 in order to honor the courageous member of the Burning Party and the Battle of Fort Sanders.

Fleming, James Phillip – Vietnam

James Fleming, was born in Sedalia, Missouri on March 12, 1943 to John H. and Dixie Fleming. His father was a career Air Force pilot who flew combat missions in the Pacific during World War II and spent decades as a Strategic Air Command "cold warrior". His father's profound influence prompted him to become an Air Force pilot.

When James was 14, his family moved to Washington State. In 1964 he married Jennifer Hansen and they would have three children. James attended college and then enlisted in the Air Force. He attended pilot training in Laredo, Texas and volunteered to fly helicopters. Then he worked, for a time, flying for the U.S. Forest Service. In June, 1968 he was deployed to Viet Nam but it was November before he flew his first combat mission.

On that very first mission a rocket-propelled grenade hit his helicopter while he was trying to bring out a reconnaissance team. Fleming managed to bring his wounded chopper out of the hostile fire and land safely in "friendly" territory. His calm actions under fire that day earned him the Silver Star.

The very next day Fleming was called to extricate a Special Operations team that had come under fire and was surrounded on three sides with a river behind them. He led a group of five helicopters to try and effect a rescue. As they arrived, one helicopter gunship was shot down requiring another chopper to break away and pick up that downed crew. Another "Huey" transport helicopter was critically low on fuel and had to return to base. Now only Fleming's Huey and one gunship were left. Both of them were almost out of fuel.

The Special Operations leader on the ground waved off the first attempt because it was too dangerous for Fleming. A second attempt was not successful either. Fleming decided that the only possible way to retrieve the men was for him to balance his huge helicopter on the riverbank while the men jumped on board. This they did and all were able to return to their forward operating base.

Then, on the very next day, Fleming rescued his wingman who had been shot down.

For his heroism, President Nixon presented James P. Fleming with the Medal of Honor. His Citation follows:

"For The President of the United States of America, in the name of Congress, takes pleasure in presenting the Medal of Honor to Captain [then First Lieutenant] James Phillip Fleming, United States Air Force, for conspicuous gallantry and intrepidity in action at the risk of his life above and beyond the call of duty while serving with the 20th Special Operations Squadron, 14th Special Operations Wing, in action near Duc Co, Republic of Vietnam, on 26 November 1968. Captain Fleming distinguished himself as the Aircraft Commander of a UH-1F transport Helicopter.

"Captain Fleming went to the aid of a six-man special forces long range reconnaissance patrol that was in danger of being overrun by a large, heavily armed hostile force. Despite the knowledge that one helicopter had been downed by intense hostile fire, Captain Fleming descended, and balanced his helicopter on a river bank with the tail boom hanging over open water. The patrol could not penetrate to the landing site and he was forced to withdraw. Dangerously low on fuel, Captain Fleming repeated his original landing maneuver. Disregarding his own safety, he remained in this exposed position. Hostile fire crashed through his windscreen as the patrol boarded his helicopter. Captain Fleming made a successful takeoff through a barrage of hostile fire and recovered safely at a forward base.

"Captain Fleming's profound concern for his fellowmen, and at the risk of his life above and beyond the call of duty are in keeping with the highest traditions of the U.S. Air Force and reflect great credit upon himself and the Armed Forces of his country."

After Vietnam, Fleming completed fixed wing training and flew the big C-141s. Later he taught at the Air Force Academy and served in many other capacities. He retired in 1996 after accumulating more than 5,000 flying hours including 450 hours flying in combat. In his dress blues, his chest shows the Silver Star, the Distinguished Flying Cross, the Air Medal with seven oak leaf clusters, and the Legion of Merit.

The Men of Forlorn Hope

You're asking what that name is all about. Forlorn Hope? Not your normal Army Rah-Rah, Hooah, Bully Good, or anything upbeat like that. Well, there was nothing upbeat about the situation that produced their valiant commitment to take on a deadly challenge.

One of the saddest, deadliest, and costliest events of the War Between the States was the Siege of Vicksburg, Mississippi. When we think of those weeks, the hunger, sickness, and privation of the residents of the city is what usually comes to mind. But their conditions built in them a strong will to resist. Each Union attack was repulsed and by May 21, 1863, Confederate losses were miniscule and Union losses stood at almost one thousand dead and wounded. Something had to change.

Beginning early in the morning of May 21, gunboats on the Mississippi began to bombard the entrenched population and 220 Union artillery pieces joined in. On the 22nd, another bombardment began but the Confederates were so solidly entrenched that all attacks were futile. That's when General Sherman called for volunteers who would run down a fortified road into almost certain death in hopes of making a breech in the Rebel lines. After the casualties of the preceding days, this squad of daredevils was given the nickname, Forlorn Hope. One blogger (wearethemighty.com) explained that these men were told, "this mission was an important one, but a "forlorn hope." The term meant it would be a disaster for them, a sacrifice of their lives for the greater good."

Only bachelors with no family at home were allowed to participate for obvious reasons. Their job was to rush forward for a quarter of a mile as a vanguard ahead of the charging infantry and carry logs (one log for two men) then hurl the logs in a position to straddle the enemy trenches. Then some of the men would throw wooden planks onto the logs and, hopefully, produce a rough wooden bridge across an eight-foot-wide trench. Then, the last group would carry scaling ladders across the "bridges" and throw them up against the earthen walls of the fortress.

It is estimated that over half of the men in Forlorn Hope went down before they even reached the ditch. The survivors then realized that they didn't have enough parts to put together any kind of bridge. Those survivors then tried to take cover in the trench while others ran back across the open field. But bullets go faster than runners.

The assault continued even without the bridges and some momentary successes were eventually reversed and the Union troops were all forced to retreat. With the artillery, the hail of bullets, and the bloody hand-to-hand fighting, the Union suffered three thousand casualties.

In spite of the fact that the attack was a failure, the bravery and willingness to sacrifice displayed by the men of Forlorn Hope cannot be denied. Many Missourians were among those gallant men. Let's learn about them.

Flynn, James Edward – Sergeant

James Flynn was born July 17, 1842 in Pittsfield, Illinois, the son of Irish immigrants. Little is known about his life until he entered military service at St. Louis at age eighteen. Two years later he was at the Siege of Vicksburg and earned the Medal of Honor for his unbelievable bravery which is described above.

When James got his discharge, he went to St. Louis and tried several different occupations and seems to have been successful in whatever he tried. In 1896, the _St. Louis Post-Dispatch_ asked him for a letter endorsing their causes in the approaching national election. They were probably surprised at the letter they received. This letter was published on September 30 of that year. The spelling, vocabulary, and punctuation are his.

"Dear Sir and Comrade:

Your favor of the 28ᵗʰ inst., asking me to join the McKinley Club received, and as you offer me some reasons why I should join your ranks, I will be explicit as to why I must refuse. My sympathies are in the cause of 'honest Government,' 'honest dollars,' and above all, 'honest men,' and I think that my record as a soldier will prove that I did my level best to uphold the Constitution. I am not only a Union soldier, but my father fought at Buena Vista, and my grandfather at the battle of New Orleans, and where he stood with 'Old Hickory' I stand – for the masses against the classes, the people against the plutocrats, the plain American citizen against the bondholder and the English money lender.

Yes, sir, I've worn the paper shoe and the shoddy coat; ate the moldy hard-tack and wormy sow-belly; was paid in depreciated paper and saw the corporations, bankers, and money sharks fatten on the woes of the country.

I cast my first vote for Abraham Lincoln and helped to free the slave, and now I see the lash of coercion laid on the backs of free-born white men. I see, after thirty years of profound peace and abundant harvest, the honest workman walk the streets and his children want for bread.

I think I am a man of fair intelligence and education and have given this question careful consideration, and I am not caught with any clap-trap of 'over-production,' 'honest dollars' or 'national integrity.' This issue is not the Republican or the Democrat, Bryan or McKinley. It is, shall the people or the syndicates rule America? Sir, I have the honor to be, yours respectfully,

James E. Flynn,
Formerly First Sergeant Co. G. 6th Missouri Infantry"

James shows up in a most unexpected way in the newspapers around Piedmont, Missouri. To understand this Piedmont incident, we need to remember the uneasiness and sometimes outright violent atmosphere in Missouri following the war. There are unsubstantiated reports of Confederate soldiers trying to make their way home and being ambushed as they came  along the Wire Road. We have seen the movies and read the books about Jesse James and "The Outlaw Josie Wales" who, as victims or perpetrators, saw no distinct ending for the conflict. Of course, arguments could be very personal and could turn very violent.

In the book, *Swindled, Wayne County's Turbulence, 1868-1904*, an incident is described in which Flynn, described as a Railroad Operator at Williamsville, a telegraph operator in Williamsville, and the owner of a hotel/saloon in Williamsville. He seems to have argued with an attorney, William H. McCown as they rode on a train. On that October 3, 1885, McCown, a "slightly intoxicated" lawyer boasted that he would kill Flynn. Arriving at Piedmont Flynn went to a barber shop for a shave and McCown went home for a double-barreled shotgun.

McCown found Flynn in the barber's chair and shot through the window at him. Flynn got powder burns on his face but no buckshot struck him. He jumped from the chair and drew his revolver. He fired striking McCown three times and then took McCown's gun from him and hit him over the head. His wounds and fractured skull were fatal. The 1910 Census shows Flynn living again in St. Louis and employed as a candy merchant. He died on New Year's Day in 1913 and is buried at the Calvary Cemetery in that city.

Frizzell, Henry F. – Corporal

Henry was born in December, 1839 in Roselle, Missouri in Madison County. His family was very poor. His parents, Jason and Odeel (Smith) Frizzell were illiterate. He told others that there were no schools in that country when he grew up so he couldn't read or write either. In fact, some record searching will show that a good deal of south Missouri was still unclaimed more than a half-century after Henry was born so it's not hard to imagine a shortage of schools and teachers.

His descendent, Jennifer Said tells us, "The attack on Fort Sumter in 1861 coupled with the promise of pay and food to eat were enough to entice a 21-year-old farmer from Fredericktown to join the Union Army. Henry Frizzell went to Pilot Knob on Aug. 6, 1861, and enlisted as a private in Company B, 6th Missouri Infantry. Henry was not a tall man, 5 feet, 6 inches. Through letters written for him, a picture emerges of a fair-haired, gray-eyed man who was born and raised on the Big St. Francis River."

Henry was in many battles during that war but we know of him because of the events at the Siege of Vicksburg. As one person put it, "Private Frizzell was at the head of his attacking force where the enemy fire was hottest and the danger the greatest." He was shot just below his right eye as he ran toward the enemy. He was captured by the Confederates and sent to an Army hospital for one week. Then he was "paroled" and sent to a Union Army hospital in Jeffersonville, Ohio.

He returned to the 6th Missouri Infantry at their camp in Alabama and fought at the battle of Chattanooga, Tenn. on Lookout Mountain. Then the 6th joined William Sherman on his March to Atlanta. Henry was at the battle of Resaca, Georgia when he was shot in the left leg above the knee. He was sent to a hospital for that but returned to his unit and remained with them until March of 1864.

On March 1, at Lynchcreek, North Carolina Frizzell was captured again but he escaped. This time he couldn't find his unit and several people seem to have told him that the war was over. So, he started walking home. This resulted in charges of desertion.

Several soldiers and former comrades came to his defense and wrote letters supporting his character.

One writer quoted Frizzell as saying, "My head hurt and my left leg, which had been wounded, gave out." Frizzell told the writer, since being shot in the head at Vicksburg, he "cannot recall important things to family and myself. I am satisfied that at times I am not in my right mind. I was laboring under this state of mind when I left my command."

One letter writer, Jonathan Williams said, "After the war he has been of weak mind, almost like an idiot and hardly of a mind to care for himself. He is very poor and destitute and the only support is from what little labor he can do."

Another man, Fielding King had enlisted in the 6th Regiment with Frizzell and seems to have known him well said, "Henry was shot on the side of the head cutting his ear and corner of the right eye at Vicksburg. When he rejoined the regiment, he never appeared to be entirely himself. . . He was a good soldier, he never shirked his duty nor tried to keep out of battle. He returned to Madison County in September of 1865."

A final writer, Thomas Holladay, said that he knew Frizzell since childhood and helped him as much as he could. He said he paid for all the cost for postage and affidavits because "he is very poor, illiterate and ignorant. His mind is weak and memory bad but he is a good citizen."

Indeed, Henry Frizzell paid a terrible price as he ran toward the Rebel lines. But the letters seemed to have helped. The dazed and injured man who fell in battle at Vicksburg saw the desertion charges dropped. Those making the decision had probably seen many other men who were just not themselves after such a battle. Henry was not only cleared of desertion charges but was reconsidered for the Medal of Honor.

Following the war, Henry returned to Madison County and tried to reside there but opportunities for employment and for healthcare were almost nil. In 1869 he married Rebecca Sinclair. It was Henry's first marriage and Rebecca's third. She had left her first husband after just three days.

He was living in Fredericktown when he received a letter advising him that the Medal of Honor was being sent through the Postal Service. He signed for it at the Post Office on August 2, 1894. Within two years Henry was hospitalized in St. Louis suffering from tuberculosis. In 1902 Henry's pension was raised from $8.00 to $10.00 per month. Frizzell's great-great-grandson Charles Dalton, said Frizzell died of consumption May 25, 1904 at City Hospital and because he was a pauper he was buried in Potter's Field. His remains have since been moved twice and now supposedly rest in Mount Lebanon Cemetery on St. Charles Rock Road. When the city sold the ground at Potter's Field in 1957, all remains were moved to Mount Lebanon Cemetery.

Footnote:

This bounty of information about Henry Frizzell would not have been available without the wonderful research of his Descendant, Jennifer Said. Thank you, Ms. Said!

Hunt, Louis T. – Private

Louis was said to have been born, 1836 in Montgomery County, Indiana. Little is known of his youth or his family. We do know that he was not yet married when he enlisted for service in the War Between the States. He was in Company H, 6th Missouri Infantry. Company H was organized in Montgomery County, Missouri so a person would have to wonder if the records might be wrong concerning Louis' place of birth. After all, if he was living in Indiana, why would he travel all the way to Central Missouri to enlist?

The 6th was part of Fremont's Army of the West and was active in several theaters of the war but especially in Tennessee. Of course this is where Louis was in the "volunteer storming party" in which he earned the Medal of Honor.

Shortly after the war's end, he seems to have made his residence in Jefferson County where he married Anna Schultz. *The Military Times* and a few other sources list his home of record as Jefferson County, Missouri. They had at least one son, Sherman, and Sherman gave them grandchildren.

Louis died March 14, 1901 at age 65 in Jefferson County & buried at St. Trinity Cemetery in Lemay, MO. His wife, Anna, as well as Sherman and some grandchildren are also buried at the St. Trinity Cemetery.

A few of the men in this book seem to have shunned the spotlight. Even though they were recognized and honored as heroes, they seem to have led quiet lives and to have left a very small paper trail in their later years. Louis Hunt was one of those men. In trying to imagine his life after the war, there are two things to keep in mind. The St. Trinity Cemetery is in St. Louis County but just a very short distance from Jefferson County. In addition to that, St. Trinity is just a few blocks away from Jefferson Barracks so it's possible that Louis worked or had a connection to that military base. For now, he remains a heroic mystery man.

Each year, the Medal of Honor Historical Society selects one recipient to have their grave marker replaced. On March 25, 2011, a special dedication service was held at St. Trinity Cemetery to honor Private Hunt with a new grave marker.

Footnote

We wish to express our gratitude to Wayne and Marilyn Schuessler, Directors, at the historic St. Trinity Cemetery.

Pearsall, Henry Platt – Corporal

Henry Pearsall was born in Wilkesville, Ohio on December 27, 1841. He was the son of Ira and Margaret (Smith) Pearsall. At some point in his life, he began to go by his middle name and most records show him as Platt Pearsall. He was twenty when the Civil War began and he enlisted in an infantry unit. He went with his company to Wheeling, West Virginia and then the Battle of Bull Run. After that, he fought at Antietam, South Mountain, and Vicksburg where he earned his Medal of Honor as part of the Forlorn Hope group.

At the famous charge of the Forlorn Hope, Platt's cap was shot off but he was not injured. After Vicksburg, his unit went with Sherman through Kentucky and Tennessee fighting at Corinth, Chattanooga, and Rocky Face Ridge. When Platt's three years were up, he re-enlisted and fought at Bentonville, North Carolina. He was at Little Rock when the war ended and he was discharged. He had escaped death during all those battles but he was left with a badly injured right arm (gunshot)  that would leave him an invalid for the rest of his life. That spring he headed north to find a farm in Missouri. By that time his parents and his brothers had all died.

He bought a farm in St. Francois County in 1866 and, in 1867, he married Margaret Ann Parks. In 1874, he joined the Pendleton Baptist Church. He stayed on that farm and in that church for the rest of his life and with his wife for the rest of her life. Together, they had two children, Ira and Ruth. As the years passed, people in the Farmington and Doe Run area began to call him Grandpa Pearsall.

It was August 14, 1894 when the Army finally recognized Platt's contribution and his bravery. They notified him that he would receive the Medal of Honor. It came in the mail with no fanfare, no ceremony, and almost no recognition. So, on March 25, 2019, veterans groups and historical societies of the area came together at his little country church to give Platt the ceremony that he never got.

Eighty-nine year old Henry Platt Pearsall Died on his farm in Doe Run, Missouri on June 18, 1931 and is buried at the Pendleton Baptist Cemetery in Doe Run.

Trogden, Howell Gilliam – Private

Howell Trogden began his life on October 2, 1840 in Cedar Falls, North Carolina. He was one of eight children born of John D. and Isabella (Hardin) Trogden. Both of his grandfathers were slaveholders and his father was an overseer. But Howell was independent-minded and often disagreed with his family about the institution of slavery. When Howell was still young, the family moved west to the bustling city of St. Louis. It was there that Howell found employment and adventure as he signed on to duties as the cabin boy on a Mississippi River steamboat.

The deckhands and other workers often argued with the boy but seem to have tolerated him with a good nature. Since he was such a fan of Abraham Lincoln, they gave him the nickname, "Abe Lincoln." He had a good life as he steamed up and down the river between New Orleans and St. Louis surrounded by interesting people, lively music, and gilded rooms. But the war came.

Howell went to Jefferson Barracks and enrolled in the Eighth Missouri Volunteers. He later claimed to have participated in sixty battles. It is clear that he fought at Shiloh, Vicksburg, and many other places on Sherman's March to the Sea. Of course the action at Vicksburg is where he earned his Medal of Honor as a member of the Volunteer Storming Party known as Forlorn Hope.

In the charge of Forlorn Hope, Howell carried his regiment's flag and fought to defend it. He planted his flag on a Confederate parapet, and defended it under intense enemy fire. He is depicted on the left with the flag in the accompanying illustration.

Twice Howell was captured by Confederates. Twice he was sentenced to be shot. Twice he managed to escape and returned to find his Regiment and fight again. In his second escape, he donned a Rebel uniform and that almost caused him to be shot by his own comrades.

When the war came to an end, Howell returned to St. Louis and mustered out. He met Helen (sometimes shown as Ellen) Mary O'Farrell and they married in 1874. Over the next sixteen years they had seven children.

No one knows why they left St. Louis but, if this writer might speculate, Howell seems to have spent his life disagreeing with people and it's possible that he just didn't get along with his neighbors. *The St. Louis Globe-Democrat* carried a report on June 24, 1881 stating that Howell G. Trogden and Ellen Trogden were in The Court of Criminal Corrections and charged with "assault to kill.

Whatever the reason, Howell took a train to Los Angeles and made a new home there. This may have been the point in time when Helen moved to Chicago. In Los Angeles Howell became known as the old man who was often on hand to disrupt the rallies of the anarchist movement. He was especially irritated on those occasions when the anarchist would burn or otherwise desecrate the American flag. After all, he had risked his life carrying that flag against an earlier domestic enemy and he wasn't going to change because of a few years.

On September 17, 1910, the seventy-year-old Howell Trogden fell from a street car and was badly injured. He stubbornly refused an ambulance ride to the hospital. He said he would "get there or know why!" As the doctor treated him, he told the following:

"*Doctor, when I was captured by the rebels once, they condemned me to be shot as a spy. After they put me in the guardhouse, they brought in another spy who had formerly been a preacher. The preacher gave up all hope and started to pray long and loud. 'Now preacher,' I said to him, 'you pray as loud as you can and I will work.' Then while he was doing his best, I worked on our ankle irons with a file I had inside a pocket knife and as you see, they didn't shoot us. Now, Doctor, you work and I will pray.*" The Los Angeles Times *reported that, "Both proved effectual and Trogden later went home."*

However, three weeks later, the San Francisco Call reported:

"*Now Trogden is about to go to the soldiers' home at Sawtelle. He is getting old and he has not much money; and he thinks he has earned his berth there. With him he will carry small baggage, but it will include precious things – a worn Army discharge which reads like a great epic and some newspaper clippings telling how Howell G. Trogden on many occasions protected from desecration his country's flag.*

Just a few weeks after that, (December 2, 1910) the old soldier died. He is buried at Calvary Cemetery in Los Angeles.

Forrest, Arthur J. – World War I

Most people who know the name of Arthur Forrest think of the highly decorated soldier from the First World War. But around Hannibal, some might think of Baseball. You see, that is why a young man who was born in St. Louis (May 1, 1895) spent most of his life in Hannibal. Even when he was very young, the boy from Humphrey Street had baseball talents that were recognized in St. Louis. An article in the _St. Louis Post-Dispatch_ tells us, Arthur Forrest, "was one of the smallest and one of the best players in the Post-Dispatch Public School Baseball League." An earlier article (May 20, 1909) said: "The smallest player on the five teams now playing in the Public School Baseball League Championship is Arthur Forrest, catcher of the Fanning School team. Forrest is 13 years old, weighs but 80 pounds, and is 4 feet, 6 inches in height. But the diminutive catcher has held his position against bigger and stronger boys on the team. He has done it because of his cleverness and his baseball head. His father, a former baseball player, began teaching the boy the rudiments of the game before he was 6 years old and he now knows all the fine points."

Originally, Arthur went to Hannibal because his father accepted a good job with the Police Department. He excelled and was a very respected policeman for many years. Arthur continued doing what he loved most – playing baseball. Hannibal has a great and colorful history with the game. They've had minor league teams like the Hannibal Cavemen, the Pilots, the Citizens and, of course, Hannibal's Cannibals. But Arthur (on the score card as Artie Forrest) was with the Hannibal Mules.

They played in a league with team including the Alton Blues, the Bloomington Bloomers, the Moline Plowboys and the Peoria Distillers. Artie was good at the game. He was a catcher and a team leader in fielding his position – even ranked higher than his teammate, Johnny Walker, who spent many years in the major leagues. Artie's batting was always respectable but his slugging percentage was outstanding. He lived at 112 South Maple in Hannibal. One newspaper article described him as weighing 155 pounds but later, in the Army, he was said to be 140 pounds fully dressed. Both accounts say that he was 5' 6" tall. He was also described as a quiet and humble young man.

Then came the World War. Arthur enlisted at Hannibal in 1918 and before the year was out, he was in France and under fire. In the book, *Thunder in the Argonne* by Douglas V. Mastriano, he describes the day when machine guns stopped the advance of American forces. Sergeant Forrest and everyone else dropped to the ground for cover. Then Sergeant Forrest began to crawl toward the enemy until they saw him and directed their fire toward him. Forrest is reported as saying, "The bullets were whizzing by me like dust in a windstorm. I was just so frightened that I didn't know what to do, so I ran as fast as I could."

To be more precise, he ran toward the enemy and tossed two grenades into the machine gun positions. Then he clubbed a German survivor with the butt of his rifle. Four Germans charged at him but he fought them off with his bayonet. Then, seeing another group of Germans about to charge at him, he dropped his rifle and began to fire his pistol into the group which sent them running. He went to where they hid and coaxed them out at gunpoint capturing six and silencing the machine guns. This action opened up the way for American troops to take possession of the high ground in the Meuse Valley. Arthur's Medal of Honor Citation gives us a precise description of what transpired that day in 1918.

> *"When the advance of his company was stopped by bursts of fire from a nest of six enemy machineguns, without being discovered, Sergeant Forrest worked his way single-handed to a point within 50 yards of the machinegun nest. Charging, single-handed, he drove out the enemy in disorder, thereby protecting the advance platoon from annihilating fire, and permitting the resumption of the advance of his company."*

As the war progressed Sergeant Forrest earned many medals for his actions including the following.

- ✪ The Croix de Guerre from France
- ✪ The Croce al Merito di Guera from Italy
- ✪ The Medal for Military Bravery from Montenegro
- ✪ The World War I Victory Medal with Three Bronze Service Stars
- ✪ The Army of Occupation of Germany Medal
- ✪ The Medaille Militaire from France
- ✪ The Medal of Honor

Of course Arthur distinguished himself in battle but he wasn't the only young man from his family who served his country well. His brother, William spent the war years as a gunner in the Navy.

In 1920 the war was over and Arthur Forrest was back in the United States. After a short stay in Hannibal, he went to Laramie, Wyoming where he landed a position as catcher and Captain on their minor league team. He did well and managed to eke out a living playing minor league ball. The height of his career was probably his time with the team at Winston-Salem in the Piedmont League. Wherever his teams traveled, his reputation (due to advertising) preceded him and he was a nice "draw" to the games.

On November 9, 1930, Arthur was in Jefferson City negotiating for the purchase of Reed Ball Park and dreaming of forming a new league of teams for the next season. But things didn't go as planned. Police found his bullet-marked car, recognized it as the one used in an earlier crime, and seized it. Of course they seized Arthur as well. Eventually they realized that he had reported the car stolen before the crime was committed and he was released and eventually got his car back.

In 1936, Arthur was back in Jefferson City. This time he had been hired to coach a football team at the State Penitentiary. His team, the Prison Panthers, were not allowed to play road games and they paid visiting teams $25 to come and play inside the prison.

Finally, being too old to make a living in sports, he returned to St. Louis and became a contact representative at the Veterans Administration office in St. Louis. He and his wife, Besse Mae, lived in a nice apartment building at 4947 Laclede Ave. That's in the fashionable Central West End and just a block east of Forest Park. He was almost seventy when, riding a city bus to work, he had a heart attack and died. He lies now at the Grand View Burial Park in Hannibal.

Trivia:

When the catcher, Artie Forrest, was playing at the ball park in Hannibal, he couldn't have known that there would be a World War. He also couldn't have known that there would be a Second World War. And he certainly couldn't have known that stadium grounds where he played would become a Prisoner of War Camp for Germans in that second great conflict.

Fout, Frederick W. – Civil War

Friederich Willhelm Fout was born on October 1, 1839 at Meissen, Germany. (Then known as Saxony) When he was about sixteen, he came with his parents to America and Friederich apprenticed as a carpenter. This was also the time that he anglicized his name to Frederick William. He worked as a carpenter and as a student until the Civil War began in 1861. Frederick enlisted as a Private in the Infantry for a three-month hitch and saw action in West Virginia at Philippi and Laurel Hill. Then he mustered out and went back to work as a carpenter.

In January of 1862, he enlisted but this time in Light Artillery and as Orderly Sergeant. Life was quiet for his unit until August when they were ordered to Harper's Ferry. There, on September 15, the battery found themselves with no officer to command them so Fout directed the fire on Bolivar Heights at Harper's Ferry. He was awarded the Medal of Honor for his actions that day but the award didn't come until over thirty years later.

He also (soon after) received a battlefield commission as 2nd Lieutenant of the Battery. In 1864 he was promoted to 1st Lieutenant and saw action in the Knoxville, Atlanta, and Nashville Campaigns. General William T. Sherman wrote that Fout and his men fired the very first shot into Atlanta. He mustered out with his entire battery in June of 1865.

His Medal of Honor Citation tells us:

"The President of the United States of America, in the name of Congress, takes pleasure in presenting the Medal of Honor to Second Lieutenant Frederick W. Fout, United States Army, for extraordinary heroism on 15 September 1862, while serving with Battery 15, Indiana Light Artillery, in action at Harpers Ferry, West Virginia. Second Lieutenant Fout voluntarily gathered the men of the battery together, re-manned the guns, which had been ordered abandoned by an officer, opened fire, and kept up the same on the enemy until after the surrender."

After the War, William became a U.S. citizen and visited Germany for a brief time. At some point on that trip, he got married. One report said that he brought the young woman back from Germany but another report has him stopping in New York and marrying the daughter of his former school teacher. Either way, she probably shared a German heritage with him.

In 1885 they made a home in St. Louis and he speculated in the manufacturing of glass. At this time, he also studied to practice law. Eventually he went to Washington, D.C. and trained as a "pension solicitor" and came back to St. Louis to practice that trade along with his legal practice. He was very successful at that and moved also into the business of developing real estate. His crowning achievement was the creation of "Fout Place" in 1892. This was a cluster of very large and fashionable homes in the area of Cook and Whittier.

Late in life, Frederick's lawyer-sons, Fred Jr. and Albert, along with another attorney, and Frederick himself were charged and disbarred. Frederick Jr. actually served four years in the State Penitentiary. They seem to have been helping themselves to yet-unclaimed property which had been intended as grants to reward Civil War veterans. Frederick W. Fout died on June 6, 1905, at 65 years-old. His remains lie at the historic Bellefontaine Cemetery in St. Louis.

Frizzell, Henry F. – Civil War

Read about Henry Frizzell in the section on **Missouri Men of Forlorn Hope,** on page 61.

Fuqua, Samuel Glenn – World War II

Samuel Fuqua was born Oct. 15, 1899 in Laddonia, Mo. Laddonia is a nice little town of a few hundred people in northeast Missouri. His father, Samuel L. Fuqua was a cattleman and banker. His mother was Lulu Belle Stevens Fuqua. Samuel's great-great-great-great-grandfather was Lieutenant William Stark, a member of the First Continental Dragoons who fought with George Washington and suffered at Valley Forge. He had a high school sweetheart, Edna Agnes Hammett, who would share his entire life. After graduating from Laddonia High School, he left for the University of Missouri. Since World War I was underway, he joined the Army ROTC program on the campus.

Soon he won an appointment to the U.S. Naval Academy at Annapolis, Maryland and, on July 1, 1919, Fuqua entered the Academy. On June 8, 1923, he graduated from Annapolis and two weeks later he married Edna Hammett, his childhood sweetheart from Laddonia. His first assignment was aboard the USS Arizona followed by assignments aboard a destroyer and another battleship. Finally, in 1930 he was assigned duties in San Francisco and Edna was able to join him for two years.

He served aboard several ships over the next several years and got his first command on December 11, 1937 as skipper of the minesweeper, USS Bittern. On February 9, 1941, he was transferred back to the first ship he ever served aboard, the USS Arizona. He was the Damage Control Officer. Edna was able to come to Hawaii which was the home base for the

Pacific Fleet and life was good for the Fuquas.

Then, on December 7, 1941, Japanese bombers, dive bombers, and torpedo bombers filled the skies and "Battleship Row" exploded. Fuqua was onboard the ship that Sunday morning and he immediately rushed to the quarterdeck which was his battle station. Just as he got there, a large bomb hit nearby and he was knocked down and stunned. The bomb penetrated several decks and started a major fire.

When he regained consciousness, Fuqua began directing the fighting of the fire and the rescue of wounded personnel. Another bomb struck the forward part of the ship, lifting the huge vessel out of the water and starting another fire that burned many men. In spite of the drastic situation Fuqua continued to direct the firefighting operations buying time so wounded men could be taken from the ship. Several people noted that Lieutenant Commander Fuqua acted in a calm, cool, and disciplined manner helping him to make "excellent judgement." This inspired other crew members and saved many lives.

It seems that everyone realized the ship was going down but they continued to struggle against the flames hoping that more crew members could be rescued. Burned and wounded men continued to emerge from below decks, the fire raged now in all parts of the ship, and enemy fighter planes had arrived and were severely strafing the decks. But the damage control team and all others still on board continued their struggle.

Eventually, Fuqua realized that he was the highest-ranking survivor aboard the doomed battleship. He continued to direct the efforts to evacuate crew members until he felt it was no longer possible to rescue anyone else. He finally left aboard the last boat to get away from the flaming, sinking, ship.

After Pearl Harbor, Fuqua served in many capacities at many ships and bases and in many Theaters of Operation. He would receive recognition for that day in 1941 with the presentation of the Medal of Honor. In his other duties as the war progressed, he won many more honors including the Legion of Merit for the planning he did and the preparations he made for the series of amphibious assaults as our Marines island hopped across the Pacific to victory.

During the course of his years in service to his country, Samuel Fuqua earned the following medals and more:

- ✪ The World War One Victory Medal (Army)
- ✪ The China Service Medal
- ✪ The American Defense Service Medal
- ✪ A Fleet Clasp
- ✪ The Asiatic-Pacific Campaign Medal

- ✪ The European-African-Middle Eastern Campaign Medal
- ✪ The American Campaign Medal
- ✪ The World War Victory Medal
- ✪ The Navy Occupation Service Medal
- ✪ An Asia Clasp
- ✪ The National Defense Service Medal
- ✪ The Philippine Liberation Medal with One Bronze Star

Rear Admiral Fuqua retired from Naval service in June of 1953. He went back to college at that time and earned a Masters Degree and Teaching Credentials. He taught in two military schools and then he and Edna moved to be near their son, grandsons and one great-grandchild.

Then, there was that day in August, 1971 when Rear Admiral Samuel Glenn Fuqua returned to Laddonia, Missouri to serve as the Grand Marshall in their Centennial Parade. Of course, the local girl, Edna (Hammett) was by his side. We don't know how many heroes have emerged from that little community in Audrain County, but they certainly had reason to be proud of the local boy who "made good," Glenn Fuqua.

In 1981, he suffered several strokes but survived. His life was different after the strokes, however. His beloved Edna died in March, 1986 after 63 years of happy married life. Samuel died a few months later passing quietly in his sleep. He is interred at the Arlington National Cemetery.

"Immediately after death, when every man stands in line and 'waits his turn,' when Papa's number was called and he stood before the Judge at that last great Mast, when his ledger was closed, there was a loud and clear *'Well Done Samuel Glenn Fugua!'*"

~ signed, Edna (Mama) Fugua

An interesting article appeared in the <u>*Chicago Tribune*</u> on July 7, 1940. At that time Samuel Fuqua was at the Great Lakes Naval Training Center (Navy Pier) in Chicago. The article is quoted here in its entirety.

Liet. Com. Samuel A. Fuqua and Liet. Com. Samuel G. Fuqua of the Great Lakes Naval Training Station.

There was the usual confusion yesterday at the Great Lakes Naval Training Station over mail and orders for the Fuquas. Dr. Samuel A. Fuqua is a lieutenant commander in the naval reserve on active duty at the station. Samuel G. Fuqua is a lieutenant commander in the regular navy and attached to Great Lakes.

Both Fuquas came to the station last Oct. 2. Both were born in Missouri. Both attended the state university there. Both married girls from Hannibal, MO. And each one has a brother named John William Fuqua. The two naval officers believe they are distant cousins.

Samuel A. is 50 years old and lives at 1506 Hood Ave. Samuel G. is 40 and lives at 317 Cory Avenue, Waukegan. Officials at the station have been informed that the confusion will end in a few weeks when Samuel A. is assigned to examine the Marines at St. Louis, MO.

Gaiennie,
Louis Rene –
Boxer Rebellion

Before we can appreciate the accomplishments of Marine Corps Private Gaiennie and his multi-national comrades, we must know a little about the Boxer Rebellion. We will try to present an overly-simplified summary of a very complicated series of events. Natural calamities and war had devastated the economy of northern China and a movement developed believing that foreigners were the cause of their problems and believing that they could gain supernatural powers through martial arts. With their rituals, they believed, they could become impervious to bullets. They called themselves the *I Ho. Ch'uan*, which meant the "Righteous and Harmonious Fists." They were intent on overthrowing the Ch'ing Dynasty and expelling foreigners. Alarmed foreigners witnessed the martial arts displays and called the rebels "Boxers."

Many Asian, European, American, and Australian companies had delegations there trading with the Chinese and many had missionaries at work throughout the country. Bitter peasants directed their anger against these foreign missionaries and their Christian converts. The Empress Dowager, Tz'u Hsi, began to secretly support the Boxers and open attacks on these groups began in 1899 and the rebellion grew. By May, 1900, Peking (Beijing) was surrounded and Tz'u Hsi publicly backed the rebels but, while she backed their cause, she tried in vain to stop their advance. As 140,000 of them marched toward the

Capitol, destroying railroads and other things in their path, the Foreigners in China became increasingly alarmed.

Finally, the ever-stronger Boxers called for all Chinese to rise up and kill the foreigners. On June 20, the German Ambassador, Baron von Ketteler was killed and other embassies came under attack. This caused the foreign delegations to draw up plans for defense which included summoning all nearby forces and combining them into one force. This resulted in a 19,000-man multinational army which they called the Eight Nation Allied Relief Force.

The Eight Nation force fought two major battles and managed to take over the Capital City on August 14. The foreigners under siege for two weeks suffered but survived. The Boxers were routed and the Empress fled to the north. In September of 1901, the "Peking Protocol" was signed, formally ending the Boxer Rebellion. The nation of China was severely punished for its failure to protect the foreigners. Lingering bitterness set the stage for the Chinese revolutions of the Twentieth Century.

Troops of the Alliance that fought against the Boxer Rebellion in China, 1900. From the left Britain, United States, Australia, India, Germany, France, Austria-Hungary, Italy, Japan.

Louis Rene Gaiennie was born into a prominent family in St. Louis (then later in Webster Groves) on June 9, 1878, and was one of seven children. They were recently arrived (1873) from New Orleans. During the War Between the States, Louis' father was a hero in the Confederate Army. When he came to Missouri, Louis' father, Captain Frank Gaiennie, was one of the incorporators of the Confederate Home at Higginsville, Missouri. He served as the Secretary of the Board of Managers for that establishment. He took a position in the Merchant's Exchange in St. Louis eventually working his way up to President in 1887.

Old timers will remember St. Louis institutions known

as the Veiled Prophet Ball and the Veiled Prophet Parade. Louis' father, Captain Frank Gaiennie, was one of the founders of that Veiled Prophet Organization. Governor Hadley appointed him to oversee the erection of a Missouri monument at the site of the Battle of Vicksburg and the heroics of the Forlorn Hope.

As a young man, Louis joined the Marine Corps and was in Asia when the Boxer Rebellion erupted. He was called as a part of the Eight Nation Allied Relief Force. Or, more specifically, he was in what the U.S. called the China Relief

Expedition. We don't know exactly what he did but his service was considered exemplary and he received commendation for that. His Medal of Honor Citation tells us only:

> *"In the presence of the enemy during the action at Peking, China, 21 July to 17 August, 1900, Gaiennie distinguished himself by meritorious conduct."*

One thing is not hard to imagine. Like so many of our military personnel in Vietnam, Korea, and the Middle East, he was surrounded by people who didn't wear uniforms and couldn't easily be identified. Thousands of miles from anything familiar, he must have felt threatened every hour of the day.

Back at home in St. Louis, Louis worked as Superintendent for the General Electric Company's warehouse on Delmar Avenue. The 1940 Census shows he and his wife, Alice, living at 555 Garden Avenue in Webster Groves. The couple had eight children but only one was living with them at that time. That son was Louis Rene Gaiennie, Jr. who was twenty-seven and may have been finishing up at medical school. That Census document also shows him to be employed as an electrical engineer.

We mentioned earlier that Gaiennie was from a prominent St. Louis family. When his son, Dr. Louis Rene Gaiennie, Jr. (USN-Reserve) was married in 1942, his bride was Beatrice Clark. Her great-great-grandfathers were Auguste Chouteau, the co-founder of St. Louis and William Clark, Territorial Governor of Missouri and the co-leader of the Lewis and Clark Expedition. She was also the niece of Rolla Wells, the Mayor of St. Louis.

Later that same year, (November 25, 1942) Louis died at his Webster Groves home. He is buried at the Calvary Cemetery in St. Louis.

Galt, Sterling Archibald – Philippine Insurrection

We've heard that war is an extension of politics. That seems to be a truism and Sterling Galt could tell us about that first hand. He was caught in a political battle that turned from platitudes to bullets. The Spanish-American War ended with the Treaty of Paris on December 10, 1898. One result of that treaty was that the former Spanish territory of the Philippines was to become a territory of the United States. To many in those islands, they were just trading one colonial power for another and that did not make them happy. An increasing number of Filipinos wanted independence.

The "Philippine Insurrection" against the United States began on February 4, 1899 with a small skirmish near Manila. That skirmish ignited an armed resistance to the American military presence. The Americans were determined to keep a foothold because of the strategic location of the islands. On the 4th of July, 1902, the Insurrection was declared over but scattered hostilities continued for another eleven years.

Sterling Galt's Medal of Honor exploits took place early in the war. On November 9, 1899, his unit was surrounded by a large band of rebels near the Pampanga River in the central part of the island of Luzon. The soldiers were trapped between that large force of rebels and the raging river. There, several miles north of Manila, the rain-swollen Pampanga kept them outnumbered and trapped.

The Army's solution was to call upon some young men with special skills and Sterling Galt was one of those. He and several other strong swimmers swam, under cover of darkness, with ropes and flags in their teeth. When they reached the other side, they were to attach the rope to trees, rocks, or other solid objects and put the flags at that distant end of the rope as a guide for the rest of the men. The others could then swim or pull themselves along using the ropes to the opposite bank.

Some swimmers drowned in the strong current. Some arrived at the far bank to find rebels concealed in the brush. Then, just as the soldiers climbed from the water, the rebels emerged and clubbed them to death. Galt was one of the few who was both able and lucky enough to complete his mission. He helped and guided several hundred men across and to safety before sunrise. For his "Distinguished Bravery and Conspicuous Gallantry in Action against Insurgents," he was awarded the Medal of Honor.

So, who was Sterling Galt? Away from the Army, what was his life before and after that night on the Pampanga River? First of all, he was born in 1866 in Taneytown, Maryland into a Scots-Irish family. He lived his first nine years on their farm in Maryland but by 1880, his family had moved to North Dakota. That is where, at twenty-three, he joined a state militia unit. At that time he was about 5 feet, 8 inches tall with a fair complexion and dark brown hair.

Sterling's paternal grandfather was from Peculiar, Missouri and, at some point while Sterling was in the Army, his parents moved to that Missouri community. There, his father became involved in many projects – especially those related to fine horses. He was the founder of the Kansas City Horse Show and served as Editor and part-owner of the *Kansas City Times* newspaper.

Nine years after Sterling Galt joined the Army, his militia unit had evolved into the 1st North Dakota Volunteer Infantry and it was with them that Private Galt was shipped to the Philippines. Galt's enlistment ran out while he was in the Philippines but he decided that he liked the Army life and he reenlisted. This time he was with the 36th Infantry, U.S. Volunteers and, according to the U.S. Census, now he held the rank of Battle Sergeant Major. He was selected to be his unit's Artificer which meant that he was charged with the maintenance of the unit's equipment.

Then, Galt and about a dozen other highly-skilled and able men were chosen as "Young Scouts." This was an early version of a "special operations unit." As the main column of soldiers would move through the swamps and jungles, these Young Scouts would move ahead serving as forward eyes and ears for the Army.

This tough-looking group of soldiers is Sterling Galt's unit in the Philippines.
Galt is seated, third from the left in the front row.

During his years in the tropics, Galt contracted malaria. This meant a medical discharge in 1901 and he was back in the United States by 1902. He was now thirty-six and working as a "sales agent" when his luck improved. He met Minette (Minnie) Ashbrook and within about a year they were married. They moved to be near Minnie's family which was from Harrisonville, Missouri and her father sold real estate in the Kansas City area with the Ashbrook Investment Company. Galt began selling real estate and insurance in Harrisonville which is where he would spend the rest of his life.

Maybe the malaria was a factor or maybe not, but Sterling was only forty-two years old when his kidneys began to malfunction. He died of nephritis in a Kansas City hospital and is buried now in Harrisonville's Orient Cemetery. For years this hero seems to have been overlooked or even forgotten. But today, the Cass County Historical Society, the Cass County Genealogical Society, and the Harrisonville veterans' organizations have taken steps to see that he is never forgotten again.

Footnote:

Our thanks to Linda Thompson of the South Cass Tribune newspaper. Sterling Galt's story would not be complete without her assistance. She also credits Harrisonville's local historian, Jackie Roberts.

Grebe, M. R. William – Civil War

Maximillian Rudolph Wilhelm von Grebe was born on August 4, 1838 in Hildesheim, Hanover which was an independent Principality but is now a part of the nation of Germany. He received his formal education at the Royal Gymnasium and at Heidelberg University. Upon completing his university education, he received his commission as a Second Lieutenant in the King's Hanoverian Guard Hussars. (light cavalry) Soon, he was promoted to First Lieutenant but, when the American Civil War began, he requested a leave of absence and came to the United States. In 1862 he arrived in New York and immediately took a train to Jefferson Barracks in St. Louis to offer his services. With this common practice, the Union Army got some good, well-trained young officers and the officers got valuable combat experience to take back to their home country.

At St. Louis, he was granted a commission as Second Lieutenant of Troop I, 4th Missouri Cavalry. Now known as William Grebe, he was a standout in his new position and was soon promoted to First Lieutenant and then Captain, commanding Troop F. At one point two young officers, Captain Grebe and Captain Hanson were leading a cavalry unit down a road near Memphis when they encountered a group of about 235 Confederates. Grebe, with about one-fourth that number, charged and routed them. The Rebels had thought they were up against a much larger division from Sherman's Army so they quickly retreated.

The other officer, Captain Ferdinand Hanson, (who also happened to be a German) opposed the charge. When the charge was successful and Captain Grebe received a great deal of praise and accolades, Hanson deeply resented it. This would become a problem before long.

Early in 1864 Grebe was transferred to serve as Aide-de-Camp to General Braxton Bragg who commanded the Army of the Tennessee. As Aide-de-Camp, Grebe had to maintain communications between the various levels of command. During battle conditions, this often involved taking communications through the most dangerous places – even across battlegrounds.

On July 22, 1864, General Judson Kilpatrick's cavalry had attacked the opposing army but had been pushed back. General J.B. McPherson sent Grebe with orders for Kilpatrick. Grebe delivered the dispatches but then volunteered to stay and participate in the coming cavalry charge. Reports say that his aggressiveness and enthusiasm inspired the other men so much that they rallied to regain the lost ground and completely routed the enemy.

During the battle, Grebe was seriously wounded in both legs but he continued to fight and actually captured the color bearer and the flag he carried. He was ordered to the rear for medical care but he remained in the fight. He continued until the battle had ended in a victory.

Less than a month later, he was at Jonesboro Georgia and was told to take a dispatch to a Union regiment that was badly needed to reinforce a section of the main battle line. Even though he was exposed to rifle and musket fire from both sides of the Flint River, he swam his horse across to deliver the orders. He next guided the regiment into position, then took the rifle from a fallen soldier and filled the empty place in the

Infantry ranks. He was said to have played an important part in turning back the Confederate attack.

Grebe was then ordered back to St. Louis for rest. It was also understood that he should lobby Missouri's Governor Hall for a promotion to Colonel and for command of his regiment, the 4th Missouri Cavalry. With him, he took letters of recommendation from General Sherman, General Logan, General Blair, General Howard, and General Sheridan. He even had a letter of commendation from President Lincoln. The President's letter is shown below:

"My grateful personal acknowledgement of the almost inestimable service you rendered this country."

"Your chivalry and daring described by the above generals and so appreciated by them and by myself, which always win the admiration of the world, are acts of absolute, indomitable courage, not needing to be emblazoned by the correspondent's pen, as they are written on the annals of the American history by your sword.

Yours very truly,

Abraham Lincoln"

You would think the promotion to command was a certainty but things don't always go as planned. It is reported that Grebe escorted the daughter of a prominent and influential politician to a theater in St. Louis. Captain Ferdinand Hanson, was there. You will remember him as the fellow German who was known by Grebe from their experience near Memphis. The two men spoke to each other but Hanson seems to have made an insulting remark to Grebe's young lady friend. Then Grebe, standing up for her honor, challenged Hanson to a duel.

One report says that the duel was fought across the Mississippi in Madison County, Illinois but that is probably not accurate. It is much more likely that it was fought in the usual place for duels, Bloody Island. This was and is a sandbar in the Mississippi River adjacent to St. Louis. Traditionally, it was in neither state and outside the laws of those two states. At the duel, they used .45 pistols and fired at each other from just twelve yards. Captain Hanson received a severe wound in his chest but survived. Grebe was not wounded. But the matter was not settled.

When the military authorities found out about the duel, Grebe, Hanson, and the two officers who had served as their Principals, were all discharged from the Army in disgrace. The most tragic part of this may have been that the four disgraced young men could not now expect to be welcomed back into their military careers in Germany. Grebe sent a letter resigning his commission in the Hanoverian Guards and realized that he could never again go home. From that point forward, he never seems to have mentioned his previous life or his family in Hanover.

Grebe went west and began a new life in Kansas City. There he met a young widow with four children. They were soon married and it became obvious to everyone that he loved his bride, Felicite, dearly and was equally devoted to the children. In 1868 William and Felicite had a daughter they called Vinnie and another they called Hettie.

The 1870 Census shows the entire family living in Kansas City and William's occupation is listed as "milkman." We can't be certain what that means. Maybe he owned a large dairy farm or a milk delivery service. At any rate, that Census shows him to be quite wealthy. That same Census shows Felicite living in St. Louis County with her daughter, Mary. It seems that the Census was conducted in Kansas City in June and then July in St. Louis. Mary was a student at the Notre Dame Academy for Young Ladies and her mother must have been there helping her to get settled.

Over the next several years, William was busy speculating and accumulating farm land. He bought land in Leavenworth County and near Bonner Springs in what would become suburban Kansas City.

In 1885 President Grant visited Kansas City and William took the opportunity to petition the President to arrange a review of his dismissal from the Army twenty-one years earlier. As a result of this, the War Department agreed to reexamine William's war record and the Secretary of War himself conducted the investigation. William was allowed to plead his case and several other men stepped forward to right a wrong.

They pointed out that the *duello* was considered a chivalrous act and was practiced commonly in the homeland of Grebe and Captain Hanson. They also called attention to the fact that, while illegal in the United States, it was still a fairly common practice here in the 1860s. They even brought the names of some high-ranking Union officers who had been involved in duels during that time period.

The decision came down that Grebe had been cashiered unjustly. His record was amended to show an honorable discharge. As they did a thorough review of his record, they even gave him a promotion to Major which helped to salve the long-standing wound. He was now able to collect a military pension based on the wounds he received during battle.

The deep investigation into William's exploits during the war convinced the War Department that he was deserving of the Medal of Honor for his actions at the Flint River in Georgia in 1864. That medal was presented to him on February 24, 1899.

A newspaper in Leavenworth, Kansas reported on an incident in William's life and it is shared here but cannot be verified as fact. The report says that William was traveling by stagecoach to Leavenworth when the stage was robbed by members of the James Gang. Jesse James is said to have ordered everyone to turn over all their money. Grebe gave the bandit $8.25. Jesse supposedly said, "Come on. You've got more. Pull off your boots."

With that, Grebe said, "You can be my boot black," and stuck his foot in Jesse's face.

James then hit Grebe in the head with his revolver and "knocked him senseless." Whether this is completely accurate might be debated but it certainly matches the audacious bravery that was the character of William Grebe.

On August 2, 1916, Felicite Grebe died and William was devastated. He decided to dispose of all his assets and retire. On Christmas Eve of that same year, he was walking down a sidewalk in Kansas City and had a fatal heart attack. He is buried at Mount Saint Mary's Cemetery in Kansas City.

The Men of The J.W. Cheeseman

There were six wooden-hulled, paddle-wheelers involved in the incident we are about to examine. I have been able to find the names of four, *The Tigress, The Prima Dona, The Venus,* and of course, *The J.W. Cheeseman. The Cheeseman* was a sternwheeler (paddles on the back) and measured about 165 feet long. She was seven years old which is fairly old since riverboats had a normal life expectancy of three to five years.

The packet, *Cheeseman,* usually worked the Yazoo, the Mississippi, and the Tennessee Rivers. But she was at the traffic jam on April 22 and was chosen as one to try and run past the Confederate gunners. Eventually she was captured by Rebel forces, her crew was taken prisoner, and the boat disabled

It is probably not possible to ever emphasize the importance of the Battle and Siege of Vicksburg. For our purposes, the number of Missourians fighting on both sides of this battle was alarming. It was truly neighbor against neighbor. Even more important was that the Confederate artillery at Vicksburg was able to control all of the river traffic on the Mississippi. This had not only military significance but enormous commercial significance as well. The guns at Vicksburg were in a position to control the flow of goods coming down the Ohio, Missouri, Arkansas, Illinois and many other rivers. In effect, the commerce of the entire middle of the continent.

As the Siege of Vicksburg dragged on, the Union Army had set up camps along the banks of the Mississippi as staging areas for an eventual attack. Disease was beginning to take a terrible toll on the soldiers bivouacked there. Steam boats loaded with supplies for those troops were jammed up and waiting for an opportunity to get past Vicksburg and resupply those units along the riverbanks. Probably the largest of these units was the 7th Missouri Infantry.

With the river bottomland filling with Union graves and the hospitals overflowing with sick soldiers, something had to be done. Some men were so hungry that they stole potatoes from a hospital and were sentenced to be stretched out and tied down with their faces up on the riverbank to make examples of them. The standoff was becoming disastrous for both sides.

So, on April 22, volunteers took six steamboats and twelve barges and, under cover of darkness, tried to steam at full speed past the Confederate artillery at Shreveport and Grand Gulf. The decks were lined with bales of cotton which offered protection from bullets but not from cannonballs. Seven officers and thirty-three enlisted men from the 7th Missouri volunteered to man the boats in the desperate run. They were placed aboard the "lead ship," *The Tigress.*

The Tigress sustained heavy damage and was fairly quickly sunk so the men of the 7th Missouri went aboard what one of the Medal of Honor recipients later described as, "a cranky little Steamer, *The Cheeseman,*" What they couldn't do on *The Tigress,* they hoped to accomplish with *The Cheeseman. The Cheeseman* ended up trying to tow a disabled *Empire City* but couldn't control that boat and had to cut her loose hoping that the current would carry her past the heavy guns.

Most of the men of the 7th Missouri were still on shore a few miles away but they didn't sleep that night being kept awake by the deep-throated roar and the flashes of the heavy cannon lighting the night sky.

The Cheeseman was hit many times by shells of all caliber. One shell tore through the steam line and took away the boat's power. The most damaging hit took out the boat's rudder and she was not able to control her direction. This was especially dangerous as the only chance of reaching safety was to go with the current and to make themselves a harder target to hit. Of course, this vastly increased the danger to a wooden-hulled boat running a course full of submerged snags and sawyers.

At a time when most men would have just "hunkered down" and hoped for the best, several infantrymen aboard *The Cheeseman* came out from their relative safety and manned the deck guns hoping to make the jobs harder for the Confederate gunners. They continued to man the artillery until they were out of range and were able to run aground in a good place to supply their troops. For their courageous actions under fire, they were recognized with the Medal of Honor.

So that's what they did as a group. Let's take a look at the individual men.

Guerin, Fitz William –
Private

Fitz W. Guerin was born March 12, 1846 in New York City. Several sources say that he was born in Ireland, specifically Dublin. It might be that he was born aboard ship as his family traveled to America. But his parents were Irish and Guerin (also spelled Geran and Gerin) is definitely an Irish surname.

By the time he was thirteen, he set out on his own. He traveled to St. Louis to where he worked for the Merrill Drug Company and for Western Union. He was fifteen when he joined the Union Army and, by the time he was seventeen, he had earned the Medal of Honor aboard *The Cheeseman.*

When this teenager joined up for the fight, he was in good company. He served under other notable St. Louis residents including William T. Sherman, Nathaniel Lyon, and U.S. Grant. We know what happened aboard *The Cheeseman* but this is the way the event was described in Guerin's Citation.

Citation

"The President of the United States of America, in the name of Congress, takes pleasure in presenting the Medal of Honor to Private Fitz W. Guerin, United States Army, for extraordinary heroism on April 28 & 29, 1863, while serving with Battery A, 1st Missouri Light Artillery, in action at Grand Gulf, Mississippi. With two comrades Private Guerin voluntarily took position on board the steamer Cheeseman, in charge of all the guns and ammunition of the battery, and remained in charge of the same for a considerable time while the steamer was unmanageable and subjected to a heavy fire from the enemy."

After the war, he returned to St. Louis and did odd jobs helping at a photographer's shop. He found a much higher-paying job stringing telegraph wire for a railroad but he loved photography and soon made his way back to that trade. Guerin went into partnership with two other men who eventually bought him out. He took that money and returned to St. Louis where he again worked for a photographer. He is quoted as saying, "There is no place like St. Louis.

In 1876 Guerin set up his own photography studio and met with moderate success. Then in 1878, he had the audacity to enter some of his work in the World's Fair in Paris. He won a prestigious award and became an overnight success.

With his reputation now established and receiving international recognition, Gueirn was several times elected President of the National Photographic Society. At his peak, he had six studios in St. Louis.

The grandest of his establishments came in 1883 when he converted the January Mansion at 12th and Washington into a fashionable studio. The St. Louis. *Globe-Democrat* reported it was the largest and most technically advanced photo studio in America. It had "a grand entrance in the Venetian style" and four floors, with departments for silvering, finishing, retouching and printing.

He was certainly a fashion photographer but he also seemed to do about anything to make a buck. He left many famous photos of children, dogs, etc. who were smoking cigarettes for tobacco advertisements. He even created a photograph of a smoking owl. He made a lot of money selling "bachelor art" which was a Victorian term for smut. But he was a wonder at building elaborate and beautiful sets as well as evoking intriguing expressions from his subjects – especially the children

Guerin was having chronic problems with his health and eventually, he could last no longer. He was in St. Louis when he suffered a fatal heart attack. His body was taken to the Bellefontaine Cemetery where he is buried with his comrades from *The Cheeseman*, Hammel and Pesch.

Hammel, Henry A. – Sergeant

Henry Hammel was another of those young men who was born in Germany (September 20, 1820) and found himself in America in time for the War Between the States. He did well in the 1st Missouri Light Artillery and, when only twenty-two, was promoted to Sergeant. As a Sergeant, he was the man in charge of the volunteer gunners aboard *The Cheeseman* as they ran past Vicksburg and Grand Gulf that April in 1863.

His Medal of Honor Citations states:

"The President of the United States of America, in the name of Congress, takes pleasure in presenting the Medal of Honor to Sergeant Henry A. Hammel, United States Army, for extraordinary heroism on April 28 & 29, 1863, while serving with Battery A, 1st Missouri Light Artillery, in action at Grand Gulf, Mississippi. With two comrades Sergeant Hammel voluntarily took position on board the steamer Cheeseman, in charge of all the guns and ammunition of the battery, and remained in charge of the same for considerable time while the steamer was unmanageable and subjected to a heavy fire from the enemy."

After combat service, some people, especially those designated to be heroes, are thrust into the limelight and some of them actually seek the limelight. Henry Hammel seems to be one of those people who prefers to drift into the background and lead a quiet life. But here is what we do know of him.

On November 17, 1866, he married Alvina Mehlhof in St. Louis. The 1880 Census tells us that he was living in St. Louis with wife and children while working in a harness shop, the Hammel Harness Company. In fact, he was a part-owner in the shop. His business partner was none other than Joseph Pesch, his comrade from The J.W. Cheeseman.

Hammel was a freemason and was President of the Gentlemen's Driving Club in 1899. Of course, driving was something different in those days before the automobile. At that time, driving clubs were private members-only organizations in which men would drive wagons, carts, or other wheeled vehicles which were horse-drawn. A modern version might be harness racing. The club's events often drew over a thousand spectators and the local newspapers posted the odds prior to the races. Hammel was usually one of the men who donated prizes for the winning entries.

Like so many fathers then and now, Henry had an irritant in his life. That came in the form of a son-in-law. Henry's will made arrangements for his entire family to be buried at the Bellefontaine Cemetery – well, not the entire family. There was one notable exception.

Henry A. Hammel died in St. Louis on November 29, 1902. He was eighty-two years old. He is buried in the Bellefontaine Cemetery (St. Louis) as are Guerin and Pesch.

Pesch, Joesph –
Private

Joseph Pesch was another of those young Prussian (German) men who came to America and played an important part in our Civil War. He was born on July 18, 1835 in Grossleiton, Prussia and his family came to America when he was seventeen. In St. Louis he worked as a stonecutter. He enrolled in the Union Army at St. Louis when he was approximately twenty-one.

Most articles or stories about Joseph Pesch neglect to mention that, soon after he enlisted, he was seriously wounded at the Battle of Wilson's Creek near Springfield. His name and home address (below) are clearly written on the records of the makeshift hospital at the St. Paul's Methodist Church.

We know about his military exploits because of the honors he earned while there. After the war, he came home to St. Louis and married Maria Mueller. In 1867, the St. Louis City Directory shows him to be employed as a "letterer." That might mean that he worked as a calligrapher or, more likely, he was a sign painter. Subsequent directories show him being a bottler of beer, a saloon keeper, and/or a merchant. Of course those could be describing three facets of the same business. Eventually, he reported his occupation as "Capitalist." He often advertised in the local German newspaper and his ads were 100% in the German language. An 1874 newspaper article tells of the night when four boys, ages 12-15, broke into Pesch's "bottled beer establishment" and stole fifteen bottles of beer and five bottles of wine.

"Capitalist" may have been another way of saying gambler. In 1879, he ran afoul of local authorities when they "busted" a gambling operation and arrested Joseph. He seems to have been just a participant and not involved in running the operation.

The most interesting occupation he ever listed was in 1889 when he described himself as "President of Hammel Harness Company. We remember that his old friend from Army days, Henry Hammel, had a harness company and that he had a partner for at least a part of that time. So, Pesch must have been the unnamed partner that Hammel mentioned in his will. He is shown to have made his home at 1811 LaSalle St. in St. Louis. This was an ornate old townhouse in the Lafayette Park Neighborhood.

Joseph Pesch was a member of the Francis Blair Post No. 1 of the Grand Army of the Republic. He was active in that organization and life in general. But old age took its toll. He suffered from "Bright's Disease" which today we might call nephritis. It's a failure of the kidneys. He died from complications from that condition at age 68 and is buried in the Bellefontaine Cemetery as are Guerin and Hammel. Joseph and Maria left four children, all of whom lived in St. Louis.

These three heroes, the men from *The J.W. Cheeseman,* were all born in other Old World countries and immigrated to the United States. They were not only instrumental in preserving their new nation but became heroes there. They were very different men before the war, comrades during the war, and chose their own paths after the terrible war. In their very different ways, they were successful all through their lives.

Gwynne, Nathaniel McClean – Civil War

Nathaniel Gwynne was one of six children born into his Welsh-American family on July 5, 1849 in Ohio. When he was still a child his family moved to Fairmount, Missouri which was a farming community but is now referred to as a "populated place." We would now probably call it a neighborhood in Independence, Missouri. We will read later that tiny Fairmount has given America two Medal of Honor recipients!

As a boy at Fairmont, Nathaniel wasn't far from Fort Osage which was a stopping off point for all of the great explorers and mountain men traveling between the Rocky Mountains and St. Louis.

On May 3, 1864, "Nat," as everyone called him, was only fourteen years old but he told a recruiter at Fairmount that he was eighteen and tried to enroll in the infantry. His parents would not consent to his underage enlistment. It seems that, somehow, he managed to enroll for three years but with some "understandings." Since he couldn't sign up in Missouri, he had returned to Ohio in hopes of joining a cavalry unit. He loved the idea of riding the horses and wearing the yellow-trimmed blue jackets. At first, they also turned him down but finally, he found a new cavalry unit forming and, without his parents' knowledge or consent, he joined as something between a follower and a mascot. Someone taught him to play the bugle and he became the company bugle boy.

Like Davy Crockett or Daniel Boone, Nathaniel Gwynne became something of a legend in his own time. As such, stories were told and the details of these stories conflicted with each other. We have noted the discrepancy in age but everyone seems to agree that the birthdate is correct and Nathaniel was not quite fifteen when he joined up.

The records conflict even more from that point onward because we know that Nathaniel did associate himself with the Army and he did travel with them but anything he did was only semi-official. His life probably consisted of a good deal of running errands, gathering firewood, doing laundry, etc.

Nat was not quite fifteen on July 30, 1864 and found himself lying in a ditch watching the carnage unfold at the Battle of Petersburg, Virginia. His company was planning a charge into the battle but his commanding officer gave Nat a direct order not to advance with the other men. He was told to stay behind. Nat's reply was "But that's not what I'm here for. I came to fight and fight I will!"

He rode into enemy fire with his comrades but the Confederate defenses were punishing and over thirty men were killed in Nat's Company C. Nat himself had his left arm crushed by a bullet below the shoulder. Soon the Northern forces were in full retreat. That's when Nat noticed that C Company's flag was still on the battleground and would, no doubt, be captured.

So, he rode to grab the flag and, holding the staff under his good arm, he carried it back to his lines. Of course, that gallant ride made him an object of even more rifle and musket fire and another bullet pierced his knee. He proved his bravery to the other men that day but his military career was over.

His Medal of Honor Citation describes briefly what Nat did that day:

> *"When about entering upon the charge, this soldier, then but 15 years old, was cautioned not to go in, as he had not been mustered. He indignantly protested and participated in the charge, his left arm being crushed by a shell and amputated soon afterward."*

The officers later decided that his bravery and example should be rewarded so they made his enlistment official and pre-dated the document way back to the first time that he had tried to enlist in Fairmount. Because of this, when he was finally checked out of the last of many hospitals, he had one less arm and a painful knee, but he also had a good deal of back pay in the bank.

As were many young men in his day, Nat was disabled but determined. He finished his education and became an attorney in Kansas City. In 1873 he married Nira Carter from Scotland County, Missouri. They were active members of the community and especially with the Grand Army of the Republic. Nat also founded and served as Captain for a militia group known as the McPherson Guards.

But his wounds grew increasingly painful and his arm sometimes discharged a fluid. Finally, just eighteen years after the battle, his body seemed full of toxins and he died. That was January 6, 1883 and Nat was only thirty-three years old. The hearse took him to the Union Cemetery in Kansas City and his gray horse followed the hearse. Symbolically, the saddle was empty and the boots and spurs were backwards in the stirrups.

On Veterans' Day, 2011, Kansas City once more recognized their former citizen and declared that day to be Nathaniel McClean Gwynne Day.

Hack, John – Civil War

John Hack was yet another of the Civil War heroes who was born in Hesse. (Germany) That was on November 26, 1842. His family came to Adrian, Michigan when he was five years old and that is where he enlisted for service. He was twenty years old when he enlisted to fight in the War Between the States. Just over five months later, he was at the Siege of Vicksburg.

We know about the men aboard The J.W. Cheeseman and we know that there were other boats and barges comprising that flotilla of emergency supplies. Private John Hack was aboard one the barges being towed past the Confederate artillery and small arms fire. Specifically, he was aboard the second of two supply barges being pulled by a steam-powered tug. Of course, this project was so dangerous that everyone involved was a volunteer.

The best description of Private Hack's experiences that night might be the article found in the *Bakersfield Californian* newspaper on January 19, 1924. Their account was taken from John's own words. He was in Bakersfield that day visiting a nephew. The article says that John was on the second of two barges being towed and, as they passed the Confederate artillery, his barge was struck and caught fire. He and the barges captain (and all of the other men) were forced off the barge by the fire. But the captain had been shot in the temple. John took the captain with him and slid down a rope into the

114

waters of the Mississippi. A bale of hay (possibly cotton) had been on the barge but had been shoved into the water away from the fire. John dragged the captain up and onto the floating bale.

John said "They were big bales then weighing about 500 pounds. They made fine rafts." They floated downstream on the hay bale until soldiers eventually came out in skiffs and picked them out of the water. The problem is that the soldiers were Confederates. John spent the rest of the war in prison camps at Vicksburg and at Richmond.

Almost immediately after the war, John married Delphina Cooley and they moved to Trenton, Missouri where he got a good job with the Rock Island Railroad. They had three children there who they named Dora, William, and Lenora. John worked as a machinist and eventually, a foreman at the Rock Island roundhouse in Trenton.

For fifteen years John served as Justice of the Peace and from that time forward, many people called him Justice Hack. Some called him Major Hack because of an honorary title the state granted to him.

In 1891, John and Delphine opened a restaurant in Trenton. It was known as the "Trenton Kitchen." A newspaper article in the *Trenton Tribune* describes the elegant rooms with oak furniture and chairs with "leather bottoms." The restaurant's main dining room had a lunch counter on one side of the room and the opposite side was a confectionary and fruit stand. John told the reporter that his place was "the finest restaurant Trenton has ever had." Of course John was still working at the railroad so it was really Delphine who operated the restaurant.

In 1900 he gambled on an out-of-state petroleum venture and lost. He had wisely held onto his farm – just in case. Because of his caution, he was able to return and take up the good life he had left.

Apparently one of the highlights of his later life was a Veterans Day, 1921 trip to Kansas City as a guest of the American Legion. There they broke ground for the beautiful War Memorial that rises above the Kansas City skyline today. He said there were thirty-eight Medals of Honor there and his was the only one from the Civil War. He told a reporter for the *Trenton Weekly Republican*, "They babied me around. They were just young fellows, boys smooth shaven and fair faces, and they looked after me every step." According to John, the hotel manager told him that. "the hotel was his home and to take everything he saw, for the stands were free and everything he cared for was for him to have."

When Delphine died, John married Emma Sigler who was sixteen years younger than him. That made her only seven years older than her oldest stepchild. But Emma lived to be ninety and was John's companion for the rest of his life.

There was an intriguing line in the Bakersfield newspaper article. After describing John as, "one of the most prominent Civil War veterans in the United States," they go on to say that he holds "the second oldest Congressional Medal of Honor in existence."

In 1931, John was 89 years old and his friends and relatives threw a huge birthday party in his honor. An article in the *Trenton Republican Times* reported that, "Mr. Hack is in splendid health and is quite active, despite his advanced age."

He died in 1933 in his home at 926 Avalon Street. He was 90. His casket was taken on a horse-drawn caisson &

buried at Maple Grove Cemetery. In the spring of 1989, Grundy County held an elaborate ceremony at John Hack's grave and dedicated a new gold-engraved stone noting his Medal of Honor status.

Footnote:

Special thanks to Laura Sue Daniels and the folks at the Jewett-Norris Library in Trenton, Grundy County. They digitized the local newspapers from the county's beginnings to the present and made it possible to find out about John Hack's life.

Hammel, Henry A. – Civil War

See the section on the Men of the J.W. Cheeseman, page 105 to read more about Henry A. Hammel.

Hatler, M. Waldo – World War I

M. Waldo Hatler was born 1894 in Bolivar but his family moved to Neosho when he was three years-old. His father was a banker, miller, and real estate developer. Waldo was often called "Boots" by his family and closest friends because of a pair of boots he used to enjoy wearing. He grew up hearing tales of adventures his parents and grandparents had enjoyed so it's no wonder that he set about having adventures on his own. His parents seemed to have given him plenty of latitude for doing that. He was three and a half years old when he first left home. On that occasion he and a cousin just decided to move back to Bolivar. Of course they didn't get very far.

In his autobiography he tells about attending a new school when he was eight years old and how, on that occasion he first came to use Gold Rope Chewing Tobacco. By the time he reached his teen years he had already operated two small businesses. In the first he sold pigeons and in the second he sold bantam chickens. The latter were often used as gamecocks. Also, by this time he learned the valuable lessons of being able to defend himself and having a good ally, just in case.

Starting at the age of fourteen, he would spend his summers traveling to other states for employment. He did his traveling in a way he called "hoboing." Like the hoboes, he would jump aboard freight cars and ride them to his destination. Sometimes he would even climb onto the moving passenger cars and ride, or even sleep, on top of the train. His favorite place to ride was on the front of the train tucked in behind the cowcatcher. On one occasion, the engineer found him and shot at him. Waldo Jumped and rolled into a switching device which injured him pretty badly. One gash, on his scalp, required twenty-one stitches to close.

We don't mean to give the wrong impression of Waldo. He was in reality a very hard-working young man, an excellent student in high school, and a key player on the school's football team. But even while he was in law school, he would spend much of his free time "riding the rails" all across the country. Finally, in 1914, he graduated from Law School and returned to Neosho and took a position in his father's bank. He never practiced law in his life.

While working in the bank, two robbers held the place up and took Waldo as a hostage. Eventually he got away from them and, stopping at one farmhouse after another, he borrowed guns and chased the men down. When he finally caught them, he was out of ammunition. But the robbers didn't know that. He brought them back to Neosho where court was in session and the men were soon on their way to the penitentiary.

The U.S. entered World War I in 1917 and Hatler tried to join the Navy but was rejected for health reasons. So, he enlisted in the Army Infantry whose need was more desperate. By 1918 he had risen to the rank of Sergeant.

He was sent to France two weeks after his induction. He claimed that by the time he arrived in Europe he still didn't know the difference between a Corporal and a Sergeant. But just a few days before the Armistice, the Army broke through the Hindenburg and Kriemhild-Stellung lines. Hatler's unit was at the Meuse River near Pouilly, France. All bridges across the river had been destroyed and area canals had been dynamited. As a result, the lowlands were flooded and the river, in places, was as much as a mile wide.

The Americans were on low ground and stalled by the Meuse River. German troops held high ground opposite them. With the German artillery on the heights and their troops entrenched along the river guarded by machine gun emplacements and other strong points, forward progress seemed impossible for the Americans.

Volunteers were called to form a reconnaissance party and Hatler and five others stepped up. Their task was to swim across the river and locate the machine guns and other emplacements. They were to collect information about troop strength, positions, and any other useful information they could find. It was mid-November and the river was bitterly cold and wide but, at nightfall, the men left their weapons and equipment behind and eased in for the crossing.

At dawn, the American sentries were greeted by two wet, shivering men who climbed out of the river near them. (Those two were the only two of the six who had left the previous evening who were able to complete their mission alive.) They brought back the information needed to cross the river on the night of Nov. 10 and the morning of Nov. 11. The Americans captured Pouilly and the heights above the river. The fighting was vicious and lives were lost but Hatler's commanding officer said they would have lost many more lives if not for the information Hatler provided.

After the war Hatler came back to Southwest Missouri and was once again active in all kinds of local activities. At one time he ran for Congress but lost that election. His reaction was to pledge to devote his time and attention to bettering the district and the problems of farmers.

In 1921, Waldo married an old friend and faithful correspondent from Neosho. Mary Ruth Miller was from the Thomas Hart Benton family. Together they traveled and enjoyed adventures of many kinds. For a time, life was very good but, according to Waldo, she spent an increasing amount of time taking extended trips with her father and she and Waldo just "drifted apart."

Through the 1920s, Waldo continued to have adventures and to make a great deal of money buying and selling real estate. Then, of course, there was the Crash, the Depression, and Waldo was left almost penniless. He started over making scented soaps and selling his product door-to-door and eventually began buying and selling real estate again in the Oklahoma oil boom country. So, while others floundered financially, Waldo made a comeback and led a comfortable life.

He did, during the Depression years, stop riding the rails. The hoboes at this time were a different group than before. They were more desperate, more violent, and there were more of them. So, instead of jumping freights, he turned to hitch-hiking from place to place. Of course he could buy a car if he wanted and he did. His favorite seems to have been a bright yellow Pierce Arrow.

Hatler's life continued much as one might expect with such a man. Along the way, he married again. She died too young but did leave him with two sons that Waldo loved dearly. Both graduated from the University of Missouri and served in the military. In 1947, Waldo had a very serious stroke but he battled back and moved on with his life – but he moved now with a cane. In 1959 he even went back to France and visited the battlefields he had known. This time, he was with his new wife, Margaret, whom he had married in 1951. Apparently she was often confused with another Margaret from Missouri, Margaret Truman.

In 1961 Waldo had another stroke and this one confined him to a wheel chair. Then several more strokes forced him into a nursing home where he finally lost a battle and died at the age of 73.

This writer could never have kept up with M. Waldo Hatler but would have loved having him as a friend. From his Tom Sawyer-style boyhood, to his financial wheeling and dealing, to his "hoboeing" adventures, he must have been one of the most interesting men to ever draw a breath.

Yet, as with many of these Medal of Honor heroes, the people of their home towns seem to have forgotten them. As I visited in Neosho, looking for the more personal information about this man, I found not even one person who was familiar with the name. And I'm not singling out Neosho. This was the case in many of the places I visited. What a shame!

I found much of the preceding information in a book, _The M Waldo Hatler Story_, an autobiography. It is hard to find but it is truly a look into the amazing life of one of the most interesting characters you would ever meet. It can be borrowed on inter-library loan from The Neosho Newton County Library.

Higgins, Thomas J. – Civil War

A young Irish couple, John and Mary Higgins, settled in a place known as Huntington in what was then known as Canada East. It was not far from Montreal and not far from the U.S. border. This couple had a son named Thomas who was destined to become an American hero. There is a question about whether Thomas was born in 1829 or 1831 but, when he was approximately twenty-four years old, (1854) he crossed the border and migrated south to Hannibal, Missouri.

One can only guess why he came to Hannibal but there were many Irish immigrants there so he may have heard from family or friends that Hannibal had opportunities. Many Irish in that day got off their ships and went straight to Hannibal to work in building the Hannibal-St. Joseph Railroad. When their work was completed, they took their accumulated wages and purchased land from the railroad in the right-of-way that had been granted by Congress. This is why Missouri has, since those days, had a good number of Irish Catholic communities in that corridor.

Thomas went to work in Hannibal as a shoemaker and later he also made boots. In 1856 he married a young Irish-born woman, Mary Galvin, and they remained in Hannibal to raise a family. In August, 1862, he crossed the river and joined the 99th Illinois Infantry and he remained for the duration of the war. This unit was a part of the Army of the Tennessee under General Grant and they were involved in the Battle of Vicksburg in the summer of 1863. We know about the assault on the implaced

Confederate line at Vicksburg. That was the time when Forlorn Hope's gallantry was on display.

But Forlorn Hope was just the vanguard for a very large assault. Thomas Higgins was a family man and was not allowed to volunteer for the Forlorn Hope. Instead, he volunteered to be the color bearer for his regiment that day. Captain Matthews described what transpired. "Private Thomas H. Higgins, a big, strong, athletic Irishman, solicited the privilege of carrying the flag for the day. I gave him permission and handed over the standard to him, telling him not to stop until he got into the Confederate works. He obeyed this order litrally."

His unit advanced at full speed toward the waiting 2nd Texas Infantry and into a wall of bullets. The 99th turned back but Thomas was carrying the regimental flag and leading the way so he didn't know the men behind him had fallen back. He kept running forward and, one of the Texans gave a wonderful description of what transpired. In the words of Private Charles I. Evans, 2nd Infantry Battalion, Waul's Texas Legion:

> *"After a most terrific cannonading of two hours, during which the very earth rocked and pulsated like a thing of life, the head of the charging column appeared above the brow of the hill, about 100 yards in front of the breast works, and, as line after line of blue came in sight over the hill, it presented the grandest spectacle the eye of a soldier ever beheld. The Texans were prepared to meet it however, for, in addition to our Springfield rifles, each man was provided with five additional smooth-bore muskets, charged with buck and ball."*

> *"When the first line was within fifty paces of the works, the order to fire ran along the trenches, and was responded to as from one gun. As fast as practiced hands could gather them up, one after another, the muskets were brought to bear. The blue lines vanished amid*

fearful slaughter. There was a cessation in the firing. And behold, through the pall of smoke which enshrouded the field, a Union flag could be seen approaching."

"As smoke was slightly lifted by the gentle May breeze, one lone soldier advanced, bravely bearing the flag toward the breast works. At least a hundred men took deliberate aim at him, and fired at point-blank range, but he never faltered. Stumbling over the bodies of his fallen comrades, he continued to advance. Suddenly, as if with one impulse, every Confederate soldier within sight of the Union color bearer seemed to be seized with the idea that the man ought not to be shot down like a dog. A hundred men dropped their guns at the same time; each of them seized their nearest neighbor by the arm and yelled at him: 'Don't shoot at that man again. He is too brave to be killed that way.' when he instantly discovered that his neighbor was yelling the same thing at him. As soon as they all understood one another, a hundred old hats and caps went up in the air, their wearers yelling at the top of their voices: 'Come on, you brave Yank, come on!' He did come, and was taken by the hand and pulled over the breast works, and when it was discovered that he was not even scratched, a hundred Texans wrung his hands and congratulated him upon his miraculous escape from death."

Of course, this color bearer was Thomas Higgins of Hannibal. It's understandable that, after the congratulations, he was arrested. General Pemberton personally interrogated Thomas about Grant's positions, troop strength, artillery, etc. Thomas pleaded ignorance of such things and was eventually taken behind the lines. A few days later he was released in a prisoner exchange and rejoined his unit. He stayed with them until the end of the war.

On April Fools' Day, 1898, Thomas Higgins was recognized with his Medal of Honor. This is somewhat appropriate when we realize who nominated him for the award. You may have guessed that it was the men of the 2nd Texas Infantry who were so impressed with his one-man charge at their ranks!

When the war finally ended, Thomas mustered out (1865) and returned to Hannibal, to his family, and to his trade as a shoe and boot maker. Life seems to have been fairly normal for him with the exception of that April Fools' Day when he received his nations' greatest honor – thanks to his enemy. Mary died on the Fourth of July, 1892 and was buried at the Holy Family Cemetery in Hannibal. Thomas followed her twenty-five years later when he was eighty-eight years old. He is also buried at the Holy Family Cemetery. His Death Certificate listed him only as senile and as a "Retired Merchant" but we know he was much more.

Holmes, William T. – Civil War

William T. was a son of James Holmes and **Kenhappage Kerenhappuch (Keith)** of Harrison County, Kentucky and later, Vermillion County, Illinois. William was born on June 7, 1846 while the family still lived in Kentucky. He was the youngest of seven children who called him Billy, and still a teenager when he joined the Union Army. In fact, he was still a teen when he earned his Medal of Honor.

He was serving in the closing days of the Civil War in Virginia as a Private in General George A. Custer's Third Cavalry. Private Holmes had been chosen for duties as the personal bodyguard for General Custer and they were chasing Lee's Confederates who were in full retreat. At one point, on April 6, 1865, two Rebel forces became separated and Custer charged into the middle ground dividing the two completely. This has come to be known as the Battle of Sailor's Creek.

As Custer's Cavalry charged in, Private Holmes dashed forward and captured the flag of the 27th Virginia Infantry. It was for this that he received the Medal of Honor. This was the last major confrontation between the armies of Lee and Grant. Lee surrendered at Appomattox Courthouse three days later.

With the war ended, Holmes returned to his parents' home and made plans to marry Sarah Johns. That took place in 1866 and, in the following year, they moved to Southwest Missouri. We are not sure why he chose to live in Missouri but his older siblings, Drucilla, Louisa, John, and Philip had moved to Bates and Jasper Counties and they may have convinced him to come. Another brother, Oliver, had already moved to Rolla. For whatever reason he came, William and Sarah lived there for their remaining fifty years and raised four children in the Joplin area.

On August 31, 1916, while visiting relatives in St. Clair County, Missouri, William died. He was seventy years old. His family buried him there in the Bean Cemetery in Appleton City. Sarah lived four more years and died in St. Louis.

Something to ponder:

Private William Holmes was the personal body guard of General Custer. Wouldn't you love to talk with Holmes about his observations and impressions of the General? Wouldn't he have some unique insights?

Holtz, August C. –
Interim

August Holtz was yet another St. Louis German who was born there on February 12, 1871. When he was twenty-five, (1896) he joined the Navy and left St. Louis for a time. On September 8, 1910, he was serving as the thirty-nine-year-old Chief Watertender on the USS North Dakota (BB-29).

She was a 20,000-ton Battleship and new to the fleet. In those days, the fleet was mostly coal-powered but the Navy was experimenting with using oil along with the coal. On that day in 1910, they were running tests and an explosion occurred instantly killing three sailors. The fire raged out-of-control and pieces of hot coal and coke were floating waist-high in the hot water. Oil was still burning above one of the boilers and it filled the engine room with smoke, fumes, and scalding steam.

At a time when it might have been prudent to run away, Holtz and five other men ran into the room to fight the fire and try to avoid another explosion. When the fires were contained, Holtz helped to search and retrieve the bodies of the men who had been killed.

August returned home to St. Louis and lived at 1407 Francis Ave. which is at the corner of Francis and Dr. Martin Luther King Drive. (In those days, Dr. King Drive was known as Easton.) This is about six blocks north of the Grand Ave. Theater District.

In April of 1917, he was called up for active duty from the reserves and served throughout World War I. He liked life in the Navy and eventually, decided to make a career of it. He was especially proud of the day he was called to the White House so President Taft could present him with the Medal of Honor.

Chief Petty Officer, August Holtz retired and he lived with his wife, Katherine for twelve more years. They raised seven children before he died on March 5, 1938. He was sixty-seven.

Howard,
James Howell –
World War II

James Howard was born in Canton (Guangzhou) China where his father worked teaching eye surgery techniques to Chinese doctors. When his father finished there, the family returned to St. Louis and John went to high school at the John Burroughs School. He intended to follow in his father's footsteps and be a medical doctor. At some point during high school, however,

he decided that he wanted to be a pilot. In 1939 he earned his wings as a naval aviator.

He served aboard the aircraft carrier USS Enterprise based at Pearl Harbor from 1939 to 1941. But early in 1941, he left the Navy to join the American Volunteer Group which was flying and fighting in Burma. This group was known popularly as the Flying Tigers. While one of the Flying Tigers, James earned the title of "Ace" by shooting down six Japanese fighters.

In 1942 the Flying Tigers were disbanded and James returned to the U.S. where he was commissioned a Captain in the Army Air Force. The following year he was promoted to Major and given command of his own fighter squadron, the 356th based in London. It was at this time that he gained the attention of the entire nation. On January 11, 1944, he became separated from his squadron and found himself alone as a swarm of thirty Luftwaffe fighters were attacking a formation of American Flying Fortresses over Oschersleben, Germany.

For more than an hour, he and his P-51 Mustang defended the bomber group from the German attackers. In that hour he shot down six confirmed enemy airplanes. The leader of the bomber formation was quoted as saying, "For sheer determination and guts, it was the greatest exhibition I've ever seen. It was a case of one lone American against what seemed to be the entire Luftwaffe. He was all over the wing, across and around it. They can't give that boy a big enough award." Of course, he was now an "Ace" in the air over Europe. He had become the first and only ace in both the European and Pacific Theaters of Operation.

The media soon gave him nicknames such as the "Mustang Whip" and the "One Man Air Force." It wasn't until later that it was known that Howard had run out of ammunition and was continuing to dive on the enemy planes in order to disrupt their attack. He was even more defenseless than the bombers he protected.

He was later promoted to Lieutenant Colonel and in June of 1944 James Howard received the Medal of Honor for his valor. In early 1945 Howard was promoted to Colonel and assigned as a Base Commander at Pinellas Army Airfield in Florida where they trained new pilots in gunnery before they were sent overseas. With the formation of the new service, the United States Air Force, James Howard was promoted to Brigadier General and given command of the 96th Bombardment Group.

After the war, General Howard remained in the Air Force Reserve and moved back to St. Louis where he took a job as Director of Aeronautics for St. Louis. This included managing Lambert Field. He also founded Howard Research which is now known as Control Data Corporation.

Looking back on his life, he was remembered by his long-time aide who said of him, "He was a real American hero, but he was also a very modest person. He was well-liked by everybody and well-received." James Howard may be best remembered for one silly response he made at an interview. Americans loved him when he told a reporter, "I seen my duty and I done it."

James Howard, the one-man air force, died on March 18, 1995 and is buried in the Arlington National Cemetery.

Howe, Orion Perseus. — Civil War

Orion Howe was born December 29, 1848 in Portage County, Ohio. His mother died when he was only four years old and his father took the family to a new home in Waukegan, Illinois. Orion's father had a sister there who offered to help with the boys. His father had a job as Professor (Band Director) in that place. He didn't spend long in Waukegan either because, when he was only twelve years old, he and his younger brother, Lyston, left and joined the Army to fight in the Civil War. Lyston was ten years old.

This is a little less outlandish when you know that Orion and his little brother were drummer boys and their father, William, was the leader of the Regimental Band. William was also a veteran of the Mexican War. When the Civil War began, he would often come to recruiting events to play his fife and he trained his two boys to accompany him on the drums. The end result was that William and his two sons were able to serve their country and remain together in the war. But after about a year and a half, William was discharged and left his two boys in the Army.

During those war years, Orion took part in fourteen battles but he is remembered best for what happened on May 19, 1863 during the Vicksburg Campaign. Colonel Oscar Malmborg sent Orion to make a dash across the battlefield with a message for General Sherman. Malmborg's men were low on ammunition and in danger of running out. Taking the message was so dangerous that he actually sent several men hoping that at least one of them would make it through the gunfire. Orion Howe was the only one of those men to survive.

One witness later wrote about what he observed. "He ran through what seemed a hailstorm of canister and musket-balls, each throwing up its little puff of dust when it struck the dry hillside. Suddenly he dropped and hearts sank, but he had only tripped. Often he stumbled, sometimes he fell prostrate, but was quickly up again and he finally disappeared from us, limping over the summit and the 55th saw him no more for several months."

He had been wounded by a mini ball in the right thigh and was dizzy because of his loss of blood. But he continued to run. He grew weak from fatigue and out of breath but he didn't stop. He delivered his message but refused attention and limped to the rear. Then he stopped to make sure the General understood the exact caliber that was needed. "They need caliber .54, General. Nothing else will work."

General Sherman's memory of the scene is this:

When the assault on Vicksburg on the 19th of May was at its height, and I was in front near the road, this lad came up to me wounded and bleeding, with a good, healthy boy's cry, "Gen. Sherman, send some cartridges to Col. Malmborg; the men are nearly all out.

"What's the matter, my boy?"

"They shot me in the leg, sir; but I can make it to the hospital. Send the cartridges right away."

Even where we stood the shots fell thick. I said I would attend to the cartridges; and off he limped. Just before he disappeared, he turned and called as loud as he could, "Caliber .54!"

One interesting note is found in Orion's own words as he granted an interview to a reporter many years after the war. He said that, as the soldiers were running low on ammunition, they began to take fewer shots at the enemy as they tried to conserve what little firepower they had. The Rebels had no such problem and they continued to pepper Orion's unit. At one point he realized that all of the dead soldiers laying on the field had guns and ammunition with them so he left his covered position and began to rob the corpses of their ammunition. (What sort of things were you doing when you were fourteen?) On that field with those corpses is where the Colonel found Orion and asked him to run the gauntlet with his message.

His heroism was rewarded with the Medal of Honor on April 23, 1896. The accompanying Citation reads: "A drummer boy, 14 years of age, and severely wounded and exposed to a heavy fire from the enemy, he persistently remained upon the field of battle until he had reported to Gen. W. T. Sherman the necessity of supplying cartridges for the use of troops under command of Colonel Malmborg."

Orion's enlistment ran out but, on Christmas Day, 1863, he reenlisted. He was discharged as a Corporal just less than a year later. Orion's story was the inspiration for a poem, popular at the time called "Calibre 54" and later a popular children's book titled "Drummer Boy: Marching to the Civil War."

General Sherman and President Lincoln got an appointment for him to the Naval Academy after West Point refused to accept someone so young. Lyston returned to Illinois and settled down in Streator where he raised a family and spent the rest of his life. Orion was a different person. He left the Naval Academy and served with the Merchant Marine. In 1867 he was aboard a ship that sank and he almost drowned. Then he joined his brother in Streator and worked as a saddle and harness maker. He didn't like that so he went to New York University's dental school and became certified as a dentist.

Orion did get married and had a son and a daughter to whom he was very close. When his wife died, he moved to be near his daughter in Springfield, Missouri. There he set up a successful dental practice and purchased a nice home at 1516 South Kimbrough. In his advertising, he called himself Dr. O. P. Howe. He spent the rest of his life there in the Queen City.

One might think that the life of a dentist might be a quiet and secure existence but things never seemed to be that way for Dr. Howe. On October 27, 1910, the eighty-two-year-old dentist was working with a patient in his dental chair when a local house painter burst through the door and, swinging a wooden chair, attacked Dr. Howe's patient who he said, "had been too familiar with his wife." The dentist ordered the attacker to leave.

The argument and the beating continued until Dr. Howe finally pulled a revolver from a drawer in the office and forced him out the door. But, before Dr. Howe could lock the door, the man attacked again and the dentist shot the attacker in the chest. The man died not long afterwards. Dr. Howe was arrested.

Much was said about murder, excessive force, protecting yourself and others, and similar concepts of law and morality. But, in the end, Dr. Howe was released and never charged. Dr. Orion Perseus Howe died January 27, 1930 and is buried at the National Cemetery in Springfield. His obituary says only that he was a veteran of the Civil War. His distinguished and unusual service is not mentioned.

Hughes, Oliver – Civil War

Oliver Hughes was born near Pall Mall, Tennessee on January 21, 1844. You may recognize the name of that tiny place on the Kentucky border. It would, in a few more years be the home of another Medal of Honor Recipient, Sergeant Alvin York, the most decorated soldier of World War I. It was also the hometown of Lt. Murl Conner who earned a Medal of Honor during WWII.

When the Civil War began, he crossed into Kentucky and joined up with the 12th Kentucky Infantry. He was with them on February 20, 1965 as they were marching near Town Creek, North Carolina and walked right into a line of Confederates with their artillery in place and waiting.

Hughes' company was caught in a fairly open area on the Wilmington-Port Fisher Road with only a few pine trees for cover. There was no protection from the cannon balls. Apparently seeing no good way out of the predicament, and believing that desperate measures were necessary, a Lt. Colonel in charge ordered his men to attack the rebels.

As the Northern infantry attacked, Cpl. Hughes saw the enemy color bearer out in front of his unit and he (Hughes) decided to capture the flag. He ran directly at the Sergeant with the flag and the Sergeant turned to fall back to his own lines. But Hughes kept on through the heavy gunfire and chased the Sergeant down. It is reported that he was within three feet of the mouth of a Confederate cannon when he finally overtook the Sergeant, killed him, and grabbed the flag. He then had to run the gauntlet back to his own company. Somehow, he survived and did bring the flag back. It was for this heroic act that Cpl. Hughes would later be awarded the Medal of Honor.

That flag of the 11th South Carolina Regiment was in the hands of the United States Army and would remain there until March 25, 1905 when it was returned by the U.S. War Department to the state of South Carolina.

At the war's conclusion, Oliver returned to his home town and Married Mary Emeline Branham. He tried farming those rocks but soon gave it up and the couple moved to the rich prairie soil of North Missouri. Here, his farming efforts paid off and he prospered. *The Macon Chronicle Herald* tells us that eventually, he farmed "several parcels of land in the Callao area, mostly northeast of town." In 1880 he saw a need for a mill and he built the first one in the area of Bevier which is also in Macon County. Also in that year, he invented and was granted a patent for a new device for coupling railroad cars together.

In October 1891, he sued the Wabash Railroad for damages they caused him. His complaint stated that the train, for which he purchased a passenger's ticket, was sold out far beyond its seating capacity. Additionally, he claimed that it arrived at his destination more than six hours later than the advertised time of arrival. If he was angry enough to file such a lawsuit, there was probably more to the story.

Oliver and Emeline had five children and adopted another. The family seemed to be respected and living well in their farming community but, with advanced age, Oliver and

Emeline moved to a new home on East Vine St. in Macon. During Christmas Week, 1910, Oliver was seated at a lunch counter in Macon when he suffered a paralyzing stroke. He remained paralyzed until he died at the Macon home of his daughter and son-in-law on January 5, 1911 and was buried next to his daughter, Cora, at the Old Callao Cemetery in Callao, Missouri.

But his story doesn't end there. In 1983, local historians began to look for Cpl. Hughes' grave. They knew that a Medal of Honor recipient was buried in Macon County but no one seemed to know just where. The land containing the cemetery had been purchased and the rich soil put to the plow. It was now private property, cropland, and off limits to outsiders. Then in 1998, after fifteen years of searching, the little cemetery was located in a field near South Locust St. in Callao. Since the family had all moved away, the cemetery had not been maintained and it was overgrown and unrecognizable.

But there, in that patch of weeds, the researchers found a large and beautiful stone placed in remembrance of Oliver and Emmeline. Other family members are buried nearby. It is still off-limits to visitors but is not likely to ever be forgotten again. Without a request from family members, a Medal of Honor stone is not available. Maybe someday . . .

Footnote:

Many thanks to Gail Shoush and everyone at the Civil War Soldiers Project of the Macon County Historical Society for their assistance in finding information about Oliver Hughes.

Hunt, Louis – Civil War

Read about Louis in the section on the Missouri Men of Forlorn Hope, page 64 to read more about Louis T. Hunt.

The Battle of Wilson's Creek

To understand and appreciate earning a Medal of Honor at Wilson's Creek, we should have a basic understanding of what the battle entailed. Firstly, it was a big battle, the largest west of the Mississippi.

The Northern forces of 5,400 men were led by General Nathaniel Lyon who had earlier presided over the two-day "Camp Jackson Affair." This was more commonly known as the "St. Louis Massacre." The night before that event Lyon had been sneaking around the Southern sympathizer's camp disguised as an old woman – bushy beard and all. Previously, he had led his troops in a massacre of Native Americans only to learn that he had attacked the wrong tribe. Then, he took his troops to seize the Capitol at Jefferson City even though Missouri had not seceded from the Union. Also there was talk of eccentric behaviors such as his stopping to eat mustard sandwiches at crucial times. In all, his sanity was very much in doubt.

This caused a strange alliance to form opposing Lyon at Wilson's Creek which even included some Northern units and others who had not sworn allegiance to the Confederacy. The "Southern" forces numbered 10,125. At battle's end the Federal troops had suffered 1,317 killed, wounded, or missing. The Confederates had 1,222. To look at it from a different angle, the Union Army suffered at 24.5% casualty rate and the Confederates 12%.

The war was young and there was no real "uniformity" of uniforms so there was a great deal of confusion. Colonel Franz Sigel mistook the gray uniforms of the Third Louisiana (Rebels) for the First Iowa (US) and his St. Louis Germans were routed. The North had sixteen cannon and the South had scrounged up fifteen. A huge number of Germans and Irish fought on both sides as well as a number of Cherokee who were unhappy with the Union Army and looked for an opportunity to fight back.

General Lyon was killed at Wilson's Creek and became the first General to die in the war. Because of this, his statues and portraits can be found in many places around Missouri. Lyon, Missouri in Franklin County is named in his honor. On August 10, 1861, the Union forces retreated to Springfield and the Confederates licked their wounds further south, William Tunnard of the Third Louisiana Infantry wrote that Wilson's Creek, "enlightened many ignorant minds as to the seriousness and fearful certainty of the contest."

The six-hour fight was not the brass buttons and bugles kind of glory that some had expected. It was mean, and ugly, and real. But Wilson's Creek was the first step in turning recruits into battle-tested veterans. For everyone participating that day, it was the beginning. For many it was the end.

Immell, Lorenzo Dow – Captain

Lorenzo Dow Immell was born June 18, 1837 in Ross County, Ohio. His parents, Jacob and Mary, had many years earlier, immigrated from Hesse, in Hamburg. (Germany) Jacob was a veteran of the War of 1812. Prior to the Civil War, Jacob and Mary brought their family to settle in Franklin County,

Missouri where Lorenzo grew to manhood.

Lorenzo entered the Army as a Private in August, 1860 when he was twenty-three. Within a year he had been promoted to Corporal and had earned the Medal of Honor. Within the next year he was commissioned First Lieutenant. (August, 1863) He mustered out in July of 1865 as a Captain of Artillery. By the end of the war he had fought in sixty battles, received four promotions for bravery and received seven wounds in those various battles.

Wilson's Creek near Springfield, Missouri is where Lorenzo Immell earned his Medal of Honor and the Presidential Citation describing his actions were very sparse:

"The President of the United States of America, in the name of Congress, takes pleasure in presenting the Medal of Honor to Corporal Lorenzo Dow Immell, United States Army, for extraordinary heroism on 10 August 1861, while serving with Company F, 2d U.S. Artillery, at Wilson's Creek, Missouri, for bravery in action."

Two witnesses give a much better account of the events of that day. William T. Williams tells us, "I remember seeing him advance between the enemy and our lines and cut loose the lead team, which had been killed, then mount the saddle horse of the swing team and save the caisson of Corporal Writtenberry's piece, which had been abandoned by all drivers and men, and I remember our whole line cheering him. I also saw him take a mule, put it in place of one of the wheel horses which had been shot, take an axe and cut a small tree, on which the piece was fast, and save the gun; also, saw him advance, under a hot fire, and get a horse belonging to the enemy. . . . Also, remember Capt. Jas. E. Totten's telling him he was the bravest man he ever saw, and that he would be rewarded."

John Kelly said, "I was a witness to an act of bravery. . .(Immell) going between the lines at short range and cutting out the dead lead team of Corporal Writtenberry's caisson, and cutting a sapling where it was lodged, and mounting the swing team and taking it out, for which act the line cheered. At close of engagement, his off-wheel horse fell fatally wounded, and Corporal (Immell) received three wounds himself. He put a mule in place of the off-wheel horse, and saved his six-pounder gun. Otherwise, it would have been abandoned."

On July 28, 1865, Lorenzo Immell mustered out along with several men from Company E and Company M of the Second Artillery. Those men were also natives of Franklin County. Goodspeed's History of the Franklin County area tells us that Lorenzo returned to farming, a trade in which he excelled. We suspect that his farm was near Spring Bluff because he served for a time as Postmaster of that community. In 1866 he married Libbie Frances Bell.

He was known as a leader with his valuable seeds and improved farm equipment. In time he opened a business selling agricultural machinery in Washington, Missouri and he was active in the Franklin County Fair Association as well as Missouri's Centennial Celebration. In 1870 Libbie was gone and Lorenzo married Caroline Rumple.

Goodspeed also tells us, "Mr. Immell is of a lively disposition, a strong friend, but quick to resent an insult; and can punish insolence with an emphasis that never needs repetition. He is fond of the society of the ladies, and takes a delight in pets in general. He is now largely engaged in the sale of all kinds of agricultural implements, in Washington, and is one of our most energetic business men."

In 1875, Caroline was dead and Lorenzo married Julia Rhodus, twenty-one years his junior. She gave him several children, five of whom survived to adulthood. He also had one child from a previous marriage. It was reported that Lorenzo was very active in the G.A.R. and, on parade days, he enjoyed marching with his uniformed son, aged 4 ½, who played the drum to keep everyone in step.

Caroline and Lorenzo spent the rest of their lives together except for her final five years as his widow. Lorenzo Dow Immell died on Halloween Day, 1912 at the age of seventy-five. He is buried in the Jefferson Barracks National Cemetery in St. Louis.

Our Thanks:

Our thanks to B. J. Chadduck of the Franklin County (Missouri) Historical Society who did some wonderful research and made it available to us all on the internet.

Johnson, Leon W. – World War II

Early in World War II Adolph Hitler moved into Romania and seized the huge Ploetsi oil fields of that nation. That petroleum was vital to his plan for European domination. Of course, the Allied forces tried to deprive him of those resources. So, in 1943, the U.S. sent bomber crews to destroy the facilities and deprive Hitler of his precious fuels and lubricants.

In Leon Johnson's formation there were six planes and they went in at an altitude of under one hundred feet in order to avoid detection and ground fire. The mission was successful but, of those six, only one bomber survived the run. Blackened and riddled with bullet holes, Johnson brought his crew and their crippled plane back to the Allied base in Libya.

Leon William Johnson was born on September 13, 1904 in Columbia, Missouri. He was the son of Francis and Minnie Johnson and had three siblings. He lived there in his early and teen years and when he was seventeen, he entered the Military Academy at West Point. He was twenty-four when he made the decision to enter the Army Air Corps and learn to fly. He was still in Flight School in

Texas when he married Lucile Taylor. Lucile gave him two daughters, Sarah and Sue. During the next several years he  served the AAC in different capacities and earned a Masters Degree in Meteorology from Cal Tech. in 1936.

Johnson continued to move upward through the ranks and to accept higher and higher levels of responsibilities. He was one of the first four flying officers of the Eighth Air Force and, in 1943, he was given command of the 44th Bombardment Group which flew the B-24 Liberators. Later he led his command into the use of the B-17 Flying Fortresses. He commanded the 14th Combat Bombardment Wing from September, 1943 through May, 1945 when the war ended.

After World War II, the U.S. Air Force was created as was their Strategic Air Command. Leon Johnson was given command of the S.A.C.'s Fifteenth Air Force. In 1948 he was tagged to lead the Third Air Force. By this time Johnson was a Major General and was constantly surrounded by officers of higher rank but he earned their respect and in 1952 he was named to head the Continental Air Command. General Johnson retired in 1961 but, later that year, he was recalled to active duty to serve with the National Security Council.

At the beginning of this piece the raid on Romania's Ploetsi oil fields was discussed. That daring raid earned Johnson the Medal of Honor. It was a dangerous undertaking even as it was planned as a surprise attack. But, as the bombers approached, they could see the sky filled with black smoke and they knew something was terribly wrong. It turned out that the 93rd Bombardment Group had already attacked that target by mistake. Now, instead of surprising the anti-aircraft gunners on the ground, the gunners were ready and waiting for any possible second attack.

In addition to that, the planes were less than a hundred feet above the ground and thick smoke was hiding the tall smokestacks and the barrage balloon cables that protected the installation. Johnson led his bomber group through the thick smoke, the flack and the explosions and they completed their mission. As mentioned earlier, five of the six planes in his group were lost. In all, 54 aircraft were lost in that raid along with 177 men. But now, Hitler had no petroleum for his fighters, bombers, tanks, and troop trucks.

And there is one more important thing about that raid. Having lost the element of surprise, Johnson and his crew had to fight off a flight of Messerschmidt Bf 109 fighter planes on their way back to Libya.

In addition to the Medal of Honor, General Johnson accumulated the Legion of Merit, the Silver Star, two Distinguished Flying Crosses and four Air Medals for his actions during his long career. There's another kind of honor that he must have enjoyed on May 17, 1957. The Richards-Gebaur Air Force Base near Belton, Missouri hosted a huge Armed Forces Day event. There were military aircraft displays, fly-overs, artillery, drill teams, and a special guest. General Leon W. Johnson was a special guest and speaker. It must have been rewarding to come back home as "the local boy who done good."

General Johnson retired a second time on April 30, 1965. Like many career military people, he settled down near a military instillation with the benefits of being surrounded by other military families and friends. Private citizens Leon and Lucile chose McClean, Virgina where he indulged in his new hobby of flower gardening. He was President of the Capitol Dahlia Society. A respiratory infection brought his demise and he died on November 10, 1997 and is buried next to Lucile at the Arlington National Cemetery.

Our Thanks:

We wish to acknowledge and thank Katherine Owens, Curator of Collections, for Missouri's State Parks. Her assistance was invaluable.

Kanell, Billie Gene – Korean War

Sad to say, Billie Gene's story was a very short one. He was born on June 21, 1931, the second of nine children of John and Iva Kannell. He attended Eugene Elementary School and the Poplar Bluff High School. As one of the older brothers of the family, he helped to look out for his younger siblings.

His sister described him as the big brother who always took care of the younger ones. He bandaged scraped knees, repaired bicycles, and resolved disputes – regular big brother stuff. He also enjoyed hunting and was an excellent shot.

Billie Gene was nineteen when the Korean War began. He signed up immediately and was assigned as a rifleman to the 25th Infantry. A lot of friends, family, and neighbors came to the train station to see Billie Gene off on the day that he left home. A few brought gifts and mementos for him.

In no time he was on board a ship for Korea and a friend from basic training was also on the ship. He was able to take a few days in Hawaii and they celebrated his twentieth birthday. Then they sailed for Japan. While in Japan, Billie wrote a letter home to tell everyone about his adventure and to let them know that he was safe. That letter would be their last contact with him.

He was supposed to attend a training school in Japan before going to Korea but, for some reason, they hurried him along and a few days later he was engaged in combat in Korea.

On his eleventh day in Korea, September 7, 1951, Billie joined two other men named Mullen and Rodriguez, all from the 2nd Infantry Division. After being with these two men for just one hour, they were sent five miles on patrol in front of the main lines to relieve another company there in the Pyongyang Province. They worked their way up a steep hill designated 717 and arrived at about 8:30 PM.

They climbed hand-over-hand with bullets whizzing around them and some other men in their company being hit. Eventually they captured an enemy bunker and settled in to the comparative safety. As the men relaxed for a few moments, they started getting to know each other and talked about their religious beliefs.

Then the enemy counterattacked. It was reported that Billie's marksmanship was effective in slowing down the enemy's advance but they eventually reached the bunker. That's when a grenade landed between the three men. Knowing that there was no time to pick it up and throw it, Billie Gene jumped on top of the grenade and it exploded. His friends were safe but the shrapnel injured Billy terribly.

But another grenade plopped into the bunker. Billie reached out and grabbed the second one and pulled it under his body to again save the lives of his new friends and comrades. His actions were as selfless as anyone's could ever be! He gave his life for his country – twice!

For his self-sacrifice that night, Private Kanell was recognized with the Medal of Honor. He is also listed on the Korean War Veterans Memorial in Washington, D.C. and a large stone marker in downtown Poplar Bluff honors his memory. In addition, a highway near his home has been named in his honor. Billie Gene's body was sent home and he is interred at the Fairdealing Cemetery in Fairdealing, Mo.

Kelley, Ova Arthur – World War II

Ova "Art" Kelley was from a family of Missouri pioneers. His ancestors came to Wright and Douglas Counties before those places were completely settled. He was born near Norwood, Missouri on March 27, 1914 to Jacob Edward Kelley and 'Ola' Viola (Crass) Owens. They lived not far from the home of a librarian who was destined to become famous also – Laura Ingalls Wilder. Life was rough in the early Ozarks and two of Art's siblings died while still very young children.

Art lived on several farms in the Norwood area while he was growing up. His father was known as a "trader" who, in addition to his farming, traded horses, livestock, and even farms. He made a good living at this but Art and his siblings were uprooted several times as they grew up. On the other hand, they were always in Wright County and never far rom Norwood.

In 1933 Art, as he was known, married Cleo Nelman Chadwell. He was nineteen and she was seventeen. They had two children, Jerry Lee and Hazel Janette. Then in October, 1943 he joined the Army.

On the night of November 26, 1944 several Japanese transport airplanes crash landed along the shore on Leyte Island in the Philippines. From two that landed safely, about thirty passengers escaped but were rounded up. Documents taken from them told of a coming major airborne assault on Leyte's airfield. Elements of the 96th Division were dispatched to defend the airfield.

The young Private, Ova Kelley was a part of that company and, until that point had been known mostly as the keeper for "Satan" a pet carabao. We would call the beast a water buffalo. Satan was being used to carry loads of ammunition for the company. But on December 4, the soldiers noticed large numbers of the enemy beginning to infiltrate the American lines. On the night of the 6th, they struck in force. For some reason, during the battle the Japanese became confused. Private Kelley thought he might be able to take advantage of the situation. He noticed that many of their rifles and carbines were jamming. So, he charged the ravine where many of them were in place. He threw several hand grenades and five of the enemy were killed. He then shot three and killed three more with his M1 rifle.

When he had emptied his clip, he grabbed a carbine and killed three more of the enemy. Many other men witnessed Kelley's actions and were inspired to join the fight. They rushed the ravine killing all of the enemy soldiers while capturing two heavy machine guns and one light machine gun. It was for this action that Ova Kelley was to be recognized with a Medal of Honor.

The Americans continued the counter attack which had been initiated by Kelley and, as they crossed the airfield runway, a sniper brought Kelley down. Two days later Art Kelley died from his wound.

Sadly, Art's story ends there. He was another of our Medal of Honor recipients who lived heroically, but lost his life in so doing. His family stayed on in Wright County and his children grew to adulthood. But more sadness was to follow. His son, Jerry Lee, drowned in St. Augustine, Florida while on his honeymoon. Art's daughter, Janette, was in Oklahoma with her husband when she was murdered by him.

Immediately after Art's death, his body was shipped home and he rests today in the Oak Grove Cemetery in Norwood, near other family members. At his hometown, in 2012 the Pvt. Ova A. Kelley-Medal of Honor Memorial Bridge was named in his honor. The nearest VFW post is in Mountain Grove and it is also named in honor of Wright County's hero.

Our Thanks:

Special thanks to Traci Bohannon and the Wright County Historical Society. They do a great job of preserving our history.

Kirby, Dennis Thomas – Civil War

Dennis Kirby was born in the September 15, 1835 in Upstate New York but his family moved to St. Louis while he was still a teenager. His family lived on Olive Street near 12th. That would be three blocks north of City Hall. When the Civil War began, he was twenty-six and in St. Louis when he organized a group of 100 men into Company E an outfit that was to become famous, the Eighth Missouri Volunteers.

Later in life he recalled that he had set up an office for recruiting men into the Eighth Missouri Volunteers. He explained further that, "A regiment of Confederates was being recruited right across the street and it was in that regiment that most of my friends enlisted."

When the Eighth Missouri was completed, it was first stationed at the St. Louis Arsenal (on Arsenal Street) and commanded by Nathanial Lyon. Kirby was elected by the other officers to serve as their Captain even though he was the youngest of them all. He served gallantly as they fought in Missouri and Kentucky and by August 3, 1863, he was promoted to Lieutenant Colonel.

On July 7, 1864 he was mustered out of the Eighth Missouri and commissioned as a full Colonel and assigned to the staff of Missouri's Governor Hall. He then served as Colonel of the Fifth Regiment of the St. Louis City Guard. By October 1, 1864, Kirby was assigned as Chief Picket Officer of the Seventh Army Corps on the staff of General Frank P. Blair. Of course, Blair would go on to become one of Missouri's most important Governors.

Kirby would eventually be named a Brevet Brigadier General.

Colonel Kirby served at the Siege of Vicksburg, Chickasaw Bayou, and on Sherman's March to the Sea. He was cited for meritorious conduct at Chickamauga Creek, Georgia, Mission Ridge, Tennessee, and Bivers Bridge, South Carolina. Kirby stayed with the Army for three years after the war but then retired from active duty.

Dennis Kirby earned his Medal of Honor at Vicksburg. His Citation tells us:

> *"The President of the United States of America, in the name of Congress, takes pleasure in presenting the Medal of Honor to Major Dennis Thomas Kirby, United States Army, for extraordinary heroism on 22 May 1863, while serving with 8th Missouri Infantry, in action at*

Vicksburg, Mississippi. Major Kirby seized the colors when the Color Bearer was killed and bore them himself in the assault. "

An interesting thing happened with Kirby long after he left the Army. You will remember that he organized a company of men and entered the service as a Captain. But someone didn't do the paperwork and his commission didn't go through. The mistake was recognized in 1882 and sent to the Senate and the President for correction. In 1893, the matter was finally concluded and General Kirby was officially appointed an Army officer and was officially a Captain for the first time – thirty years after the fact.

General Dennis T. Kirby died on April 18, 1922 and lies buried at the Arlington National Cemetery.

Lee, Hubert L. – Korea

We don't hear much about Arburg, Missouri. It's literally just a wide spot on the road. It's never been a city, a town, or even a post office. It's just a community in the country not too far from Dexter. As one man said, "Only me and one old Indian Chief know about this place." But, Arburg gave America a Hero.

Hubert Lee was one of five sons of Charles and Beulah Lee. Charles was a fireman working for the St. Louis Southwestern Railway Company. (Now known as the Union Pacific.) It was the nature of railroad jobs that workers get transferred a lot and that was the case with Charles Lee. Because of that, young Hubert grew up in Missouri, Arkansas, and Mississippi.

When Hubert eventually joined the Army he was 31 years old and looked like a tough country farm hand. One reporter described him well. "Heroes come in assorted sizes, and Lee is of the sawed-off variety. He reminds you of James Cagney at the movies except for the drawl. He's a short, barrel-chested guy with a big, powerful arms and hands, is 5 feet, 4¼ and weighs 165."

Another reporter described him as an old soldier with a hard-boiled veneer. Someone else said he was "florid-faced." We can feel assured that he was a tough little guy – the one you would always want to have on your side.

Lee was inducted into the Army just prior to World War II (May 1939) and found a job he liked. He fought in North Africa and Italy. He served with distinction, and was awarded a Bronze Star and Silver Star for heroism.

By the time Korea erupted in 1950, he was a Master Sergeant and on February 1, 1951, his Company I, along wih a contingent of French soldiers, was holding a position near Ip'o-ri, Korea, when they were attacked by a large force of Chinese Communist soldiers. Company I was driven from its position, and Lee's platoon leader was wounded.

As Lee said later, "There wasn't anyone left to take over." So, he stepped up. He took command of the survivors of his platoon and counter attacked their original position which was now occupied by the Chinese troops. Advancing to within twenty-five yards of their goal, Lee was wounded in the leg by grenade fragments but refused medical attention and continued the attack. The small group of U.S. troops was forced to retreat five times, but each time Lee would rally the remaining soldiers to move forward again.

During the final attack, an exploding grenade caused serious wounds in both legs, but the Master Sergeant began crawling forward, calling his men to join him as he rose to his knees to fire on the enemy. Wounded a third time by small-arms fire, Lee continued crawling forward and leading his troops toward their objective. All but ten of Lee's men were either killed or incapacitated by wounds. The Americans lost twenty-two dead and fifty-five wounded while inflicting eighty-three dead and around 200 wounded on the Chinese troops. Or, as the

Medal of Honor Citation states, Lee's "intrepid leadership and determination led to the destruction of 83 of the enemy and withdrawal of the remainder, and was a vital factor in stopping the enemy attack,"

Lee recovered from his wounds and returned to duty on May 26, 1951. He and another soldier each received a Medal of Honor from President Harry Truman in a White House ceremony on January 29, 1952.

After the Korean War, Lee remained in the army, and served for a while in Alaska. He married Dorothy B. Ream in Anchorage on April 19, 1956. He retired from the army in 1958 and worked civil service jobs in Alaska for a while before returning to warmer climes.

There was a time when Hubert Lee discovered what so many other members of the military have discovered – civilian jobs can be very hard to find. So he enrolled in an electronics program with help from the GI Bill. Even then, he had trouble finding employment. Finally, a newspaper article reached a man in Detroit who contacted Lee and offered him a job repairing radio and electronic equipment.

By all accounts Herbert's last years were good ones. He didn't feel comfortable in the limelight and, while he would speak to school groups or civic clubs, he preferred to spend his time with his family or his fishing pole. One person who knew him in those later years said, "He loved to fish and was a quite unassuming person. Though he was wounded several times in the war, he showed no outward sign of any damage, limp or other ailment. You would not know the great and heroic things he had done by meeting him."

Master Sergeant Hubert L. Lee died there of a heart attack on November 5, 1982 and is buried near other members of the Lee family in Stoneville-Leland Cemetery in Mississippi.

Lindbergh, Charles Augustus – Special Non-Combatant

Our most famous Medal of Honor recipient is also our most controversial. Some people would deny that he belongs in this Missouri collection of military heroes because he is not from Missouri. Others would deny him because his heroic accomplishment was not done in military service. So, let's look at those two things before we go on.

If Charles Lindbergh did not live in Missouri, then where did he live? He was born and spent a few years living with his family in Michigan. Then their house burned and the family decided it was time to move to Minnesota. His father was elected to Congress from that place and went to live in Washington, D.C. Since there were no airlines to go back and forth between home, the family lived most of the year in Washington and that is where Charles spent many of his early years.

Lindbergh had, for much of his young life, a strong fascination with the flying machines and at his earliest opportunity, he enrolled in the Army's flight school. After graduating from the Army's pilot training in 1925, he was commissioned as a 2nd Lieutenant and, for the first time in his life, he chose where his new home would be. He chose to move to St. Louis, the hotbed of aviation.

In St. Louis, he formed the air wing of the Missouri National Guard and, to this very day, their planes proclaim on each fuselage, "Lindbergh's Own." The National Guard did not offer full-time employment so he worked for the Robertson Aircraft Corporation to fly passengers and to give flying lessons. One of his routine passengers was a St. Louis attorney, Eddie O'Hare, who frequently went to Chicago to meet with his boss, Al Capone. Eddie's son, Butch O'Hare would go along on the flights as often as possible and Butch became a Medal of Honor pilot whom we will discuss in later pages.

Lindbergh's main source of income after 1926 was his job flying the U.S. Mail from St. Louis to Chicago and back. As Robertson's chief pilot, he was responsible for scheduling and plotting the route and for making the actual flights. Flying the mail was a dangerous job. He had to deal with poor weather, nighttime flying, and fatigue. Walking away from his many crashes earned him the nickname, Lucky Lindy. But, as he made these challenging open-cockpit flights, he gained experience and improved his flying skills.

The likeable young man made many important friends during his Missouri years including Albert Bond Lambert, Harold M. Bixby, Frank H. Robertson, William B. Robertson, Harry F. Knight, Harry H. Knight, J.D. Wooster Lambert, E. Lansing Ray, and Earl C. Thompson. These men would come to be known as "the St. Louis backers." They paid for the famous *Spirit of St. Louis* monoplane. They were, in fact, who the plane was named for.

Lindbergh lived in St. Louis for four years prior to his solo trans-Atlantic flight. Always wanting to be near the hub of aviation activity, he took a room in the boarding house directly across from his employer, Robertson Aircraft

Corporation. You can see the white house in this photograph furnished by the Missouri historian, Joe Sonderman.

So, what about his time after the famous flight across the Atlantic? Where did Lindbergh choose to live then? The 1930 Census shows Charles Lindbergh and his new wife Anne, living at 320 Union Boulevard in St. Louis. Once again, the young pilot (now the world's greatest hero) could have lived anywhere but he chose St. Louis. We all know that he later bounced from place-to-place living in England, New Jersey, and Hawaii. But we believe that Missouri has as much claim to the young hero as any other state. This is where he honed his flying skills and where he lived when he accomplished his Medal of Honor feat.

So, what then of the criticism that his medal was not earned in battle? That fact is very obvious and the medal was created to reward valor in combat. Some of the justifications follow:

1. He was not a member of any of the armed services. Actually, as an officer in the Missouri Air National Guard, he was a reserve officer in the Army Air Corps. He eventually rose to the rank of Colonel.

2. His feat of bravery was not in a battle. That is very true but he was a hero and the public demanded that Congress recognize him as such.

3. He was not in uniform when he made that famous and dangerous flight. This is also true but the military really didn't have the appropriate flight suits at that time and wearing any conventional uniform was out of the question in the subarctic conditions of the northern path of his flight.

4. He was anti-American and was once called "America's leading Nazi." Yes, he was called names but was never anti-American. He did warn that our depression-torn America might not be able to survive a fight with the advanced weapons of Hitler's more modern military. Facing facts and calling for caution is not a traitorous act. Of course, when the fighting began, he offered his services and was used by our military in many ways.

Lindbergh went to work for Henry Ford as a consultant as the Ford factories produced the B-24 bombers. He also worked for the United Aircraft Corporation to develop the F-4U Corsair used by the Navy and Marines. Somehow, he even flew fifty wartime missions in the Pacific.

To this writer, Lindbergh's receiving of the Medal of Honor boils down to the fact that Americans were demanding the highest form of recognition for young Mr. Lindbergh. The Medal of Honor is the highest.

So, "by special act of Congress," the award was presented to Lindbergh.

For all the reasons mentioned above, Congress did revoke the medals of Lindbergh and several other people including Buffalo Bill Cody and other civilian scouts who were only employed by the army but were not enlisted members of the military. The Congress later reversed its policy and reinstated the medals to those individuals. Lindbergh's Medal of Honor is on display at the Missouri History Museum in Forest park, just a few blocks from the apartment that Charles and Anne shared as newlyweds.

It probably serves no purpose to try and detail all the facets of this man's complicated life. We all know that he was a great hero, a great diplomatic representative for our country, a loving husband and a grief-stricken father when his son was kidnapped and murdered. We know about his warnings of German might and his German family. We remember his reclusive lifestyle on the Island of Maui where he and Anne died and are buried. All of the details are highly-documented and readily available.

The conclusion is this. Charles Lindbergh was the most famous of all our Medal of Honor recipients as well as the most controversial. And yes, he did belong to Missouri as much as any other state.

Our Thanks:

Thanks to Joe Sonderman and Mike Bender for their contributions to our understanding of the complex life of Charles Lindberg.

Long, Charles Richard –

Korean War

Charles Richard Long was known by almost everyone as Richard. But his family called him "Buddy." He was born on December 10, 1923 as the middle child of three. His parents were Lois and Fritz Long from the Mount Washington neighborhood in Independence, Missouri. Coincidentally, Richards home was only a few blocks away from the Fairmount neighborhood where the Medal of Honor recipient, Nathaniel Gwynne had lived.

As Long grew up, many of his years were during the Great Depression and his family was at least as poor as everyone else. To make ends meet, the family took in borders so there were nine people living in his small house – with only one bathroom! Richard added to the family income by "throwing" the *Kansas City Star* and the *Fairmount Inter-City News*. His sister Edith remembered, "Back then, delivering *The Kansas City Star* was on rainy days, you walked and porched them." He also sold soda pop at the Mount Washington junction in Independence. He enjoyed singing in a quartet called "The Four Wrong Fonts."

In 1941 he graduated from Northeast High School then followed his brother's example and joined the Army. He fought  in the Battle of the Bulge during World War II then remained in the U.S. Army Reserves following the War. "He wanted to re-enter active duty as an escort, his sister said, though he was denied because of his high blood pressure.

In spite of all, the conflict broke out in Korea. By February, 1951, he was in Korea serving as a Sergeant with the 2nd Infantry Division. In the early morning of the 12th, he was on Hill 300 near Hoengseong and acting as a forward observer for the company's mortar platoon.

They came under attack by a numerically superior force. He was ordered to withdraw, but voluntarily stayed at his forward post, holding off the enemy with his M1 and hand grenades. Using his radio, he continued to direct mortar fire. His last radio message said that he was out of ammunition and he called for a 40-round mortar strike near his position. He was surrounded and killed soon after.

For this gallantry, he was posthumously awarded the Medal of Honor a year later, on February 1, 1952. The medal was presented to his family by President Truman.

Long's official Citation reads:

> *"Sgt. Long, a member of Company M, distinguished himself by conspicuous gallantry and intrepidity above and beyond the call of duty in action against an armed enemy of the United Nations. When Company M, in a defensive perimeter on Hill 300, was viciously attacked by a numerically superior hostile force at approximately 0300 hours and ordered to withdraw, Sgt. Long, a forward observer for the mortar platoon, voluntarily remained at his post to provide cover by directing mortar fire on the enemy. Maintaining radio contact with his platoon, Sgt. Long coolly directed accurate mortar fire on the advancing foe. He continued firing his carbine and throwing handgrenades until his position was surrounded and he was mortally wounded. Sgt. Long's inspirational, valorous action halted the onslaught, exacted a heavy toll of enemy casualties, and enabled his company to withdraw, reorganize, counterattack, and regain the hill strongpoint. His unflinching courage and noble self-sacrifice reflect the highest credit on himself and are in keeping with the honored traditions of the military service."*

Aged 27 at his death, Long was buried at Mount Washington Forever Cemetery in his hometown of Independence. His name can now be seen at military facilities in the U.S. and in Korea. Camp Long near Wonju, South Korea is named for him as is the Charles R. Long Army Reserve Center in Independence. The Truman Memorial Building in Independence has a special display area honoring Long. A bridge on U.S. Highway 24 near his home has been named in his honor. A school at Camp Humphreys in South Korea has been named the Charles R. Long Elementary School.

When so many heroes seem to have been forgotten, Richard Long is remembered for his inspirational actions.

McGuire, Fred Henry – Spanish-American War

Gordonville is just a little place. Today it has about 400 residents and it sits about six miles from Jackson and about ten miles from Cape Girardeau. But if Chief Pharmacist's Mate Fred McGuire is any indication, they must grow them rugged around there.

Fred was born on November 7, 1890 at his father's farm. The _Weekly Tribune_ in Cape Girardeau described the McGuires as, "one of the county's most prominent families." By the time he was seventeen, he was living in Mountain Grove and had already been granted a Certificate as a Registered Druggist for the state of Missouri. He lived in Mt. Grove at that time. On December 3, 1913, he married Florence Reed of Laflin, MO and two years later their daughter, Geraldine, was born.

When he was nineteen, he joined the Navy and went right to basic training. He rose from Seaman to Hospital Apprentice and then to Chief Pharmacist's Mate. In 1911 he was serving aboard the U.S.S. Pampanga. She was originally a

Spanish gunboat but had been captured by the U.S. Navy and outfitted as a U.S. vessel.

In her new life, the Pampanga first saw duties with the Army near Corregidor Island but was returned to the Navy in 1910. The day she was re-commissioned as a naval vessel, in April, 1911, young Fred McGuire was aboard. They were assigned to patrol duty off the coast of Basilan Island in the Philippines. They were to help suppress the growing resistance to the American presence in the archipelago.

One of the centers of enemy activity was the village of Mundang so, on September 24, 1911, a small shore party was sent inland to the village. Fred McGuire was their medic. The team was moving through tall grass about one hundred yards from the village when they came under heavy fire followed by an assault. His commanding officer was hit and went down so McGuire went to his aid. He used his rifle until he ran out of ammunition and then he used it as a club. He continued this hand-to-hand fighting until additional Americans could arrive.

McGuire himself was wounded but he ministered to the needs of his commanding officer and the other fallen troops and no doubt saved the lives of at least two men that day and probably more.

His Medal of Honor Citation describes his actions:

"While attached to the U.S.S. Pampang, McGuire was one of a shore party moving in to capture Mundang, on the island of Basilan, Philippine Islands, on the morning of 24 September 1911. Ordered to take station within 100 yards of a group of nipa huts close to the trail, McGuire advanced and stood guard as the leader and his scout party first searched the surrounding deep grasses, then moved into the open area before the huts.

Instantly enemy Moros opened point-blank fire on the exposed men and approximately 20 Moros charged the small group from inside the huts and from other concealed positions. McGuire, responding to the calls for help, was one of the first on the scene. After emptying his rifle into the attackers, he closed in with rifle, using it as a club to wage fierce battle until his comrades arrived on the field, when he rallied to the aid of his dying leader and other wounded.

Although himself wounded, McGuire ministered tirelessly and efficiently to those who had been struck down, thereby saving the lives of 2 who otherwise might have succumbed to enemy-inflicted wounds."

Fred McGuire retired from the Navy in 1939 but was recalled for active duty in World War II. He was stationed in Navy hospitals during that war. He was able to retire again in October, 1945 and returned to Mountain Grove, Missouri. On September 12, 1946, Governor Donnelley drove down to Mountain Grove and gave an inspiring speech in honor of McGuire. Fred McGuire died of a heart attack in Mountain Grove at age sixty-seven and is buried at the National Cemetery in Springfield, Missouri.

Merrifield, James K. – Civil War

James K. Merrifield was born on August 20, 1844 to John and Jane Widener Merrifield in Pennsylvania. The 1850 Census shows James living with his parents and his father is listed as a merchant. At some time within the next seven years, his mother died. In 1860 James' father is enumerated as a physician and they are living with James' new step-mother, Charlotte. August 8, 1862 found seventeen-year-old James way over in Manilius, Illinois and joining the 88th Illinois Infantry.

Earlier, in the story of *Captain Freeman Davis,* we discussed the perceived importance of protecting your unit's battle flag and the pride in capturing a flag from the enemy. Capturing flags is how James Merrifield earned his Medal of Honor.

He was serving with Sherman's army as they marched to the sea in order to divide and conquer the Confederacy. Then he returned with Schofield and fought in the battles at Franklin and Nashville. The Citation that came with his Medal of Honor is very sparse in its description of the event, saying only:

> *"The President of the United States of America, in the name of Congress, takes pleasure in presenting the Medal of Honor to Corporal James K. Merrifield, United States Army, for extraordinary heroism on 30 November 1864, while serving with Company C, 88th Illinois Infantry, in action at Franklin, Tennessee. Corporal Merrifield captured two battle flags from the enemy and returned with them to his own lines."*

It's a more interesting story when told in his own words. This is how the event was related in the *Mower County Transcript* in Lansing, Minnesota in 1909. It is reprinted from an article in the publication called the *Confederate Veteran*:

"After a charge by Gen. Cockrill's Missouri brigade, I ran out over the works about 100 feet where I had spotted a flag go down. I picked up the flag, pulled it off the staff and put it in my pocket. A fine-looking officer lying there covered with dead bodies asked me if I would remove them from his leg, as he was wounded in the knee. I got his leg free. Then he asked me for a drink out of my canteen. I leaned over and told him to drink. While he was drinking, he asked me to unbuckle his sword belt which I did. Just then I heard the wisp of a bullet, and looking up, I saw another line almost 100 feet distant advancing. I turned and ran to our works, taking the belt and sword with me. These I presented in the Historical Society in St. Louis through Gen. Harding of Jefferson City.

"The flag was of the First Missouri Infantry and was destroyed in the big fire in Chicago. The sword was the property of Col. Hugh Garland commanding the first Missouri Regiment in that battle. Col. Garland was undoubtedly killed where he lay after I left him because he was in the line of the firing. I have no doubt that I was the last person to whom Col. Garland ever spoke. I have often wondered if any of his relatives were living. If so, I wish I could see them. I was glad to be able to give him a drink of water."

Shortly after Merrifield's comments were published, he received a letter from an ex-Confederate. The letter came from Washington, (Washington, Missouri or D.C. or Washington state?) and it says:

"Dear Sir: I notice in the *Confederate Veteran* a very interesting article under the head of "The (?) at Franklin" which reminds me so forcibly of what I saw and heard myself on that bloody battle field November 30, 1864. I was Captain of Company B, Second and Sixth Missouri Infantry, General Cockrell's brigade. In the famous charge made by the Missouri brigade I was seriously wounded in my right leg (which was amputated the next day on the field) near the federal breastworks close to the cotton gin, and not far from the Carter house. My wound was so serious that I could not crawl or get away and while thus prostrated on the ground I was shot through the forearm shattering both bones and a few minutes thereafter I was again shot in my left shoulder."

'In this awful condition, with my clothes saturated with blood, and with hundreds of dead and wounded confederate soldiers lying (?) in a heap about me, I beheld the dead body of Col. Hugh Garland commanding the First Missouri regiment in this battle, who was killed by a second shot, and while prostrated on the ground, and many other wounded confederates were killed all around me while lying on the ground (?) in their own blood. I was not more than six feet from Col. Garland whom a federal soldier (to me unknown) did give Col Garland water from his canteen and straighten him out on the ground relieving him somewhat from the weight of other poor dying comrades."

There is more from this letter but the sections above serve to show that there was much more involved than just the taking of someone's flag. It also shows that, during the horrific events in a battle, there can be moments of humanity and those moments are remembered. The Confederate writer was Captain J.M. Hickey, Company B and Sixth Missouri Infantry, C.S.A.

This would have been John Hickey from Howard County, Missouri.

James Merrifield mustered out of the Army in Nashville on June 9, 1865. He went straight to Great Bend, Pennsylvania where he married Miss Rhoda Crandall. After a time, James went to St. Louis where he took a job with the Missouri Pacific Railroad. Then Rhoda joined him in St. Louis.

By 1870 he was one of the line's top conductors. In 1875 James earned a nickname that would stay with him for the rest of his life. He would be forever known as "Tornado Jim." The *Sedalia Weekly Democrat* newspaper tells how it happened.

> *"He got the name Tornado Jim from no violence of temperament, for a more quiet, gentlemanly man never took up tickets in a car, albeit he had plenty of true courage when it came in need. His train on Lexington Branch of the Missouri Pacific railway was completely blown from the track and wrecked in a fearful tornado a number of years ago, and since he has always been known as Tornado Jim."*

It is also said that he saw the inevitable collision of the funnel and the train and somehow led many passengers to safety before the train was destroyed. At any rate, he had another colorful chapter in his fascinating life.

The 1880 Census finds James and Rhoda living in Lexington, Missouri with their three-year-old son, Walter. At that time his duties involved running one of the trains between St. Louis and Kansas City. But even though he worked for the Missouri Pacific for forty-two years, his life was one of constant change. In 1890, he ran for Railroad Commissioner as the Democrat nominee but that was a year of a Republican sweep.

Then, in 1896, it must have been one of his best days as the Medal of Honor arrived in the mail. In 1900 the Census finds him back in St. Louis living with Rhoda as boarders with a Winkoop family. Their twenty-three-year-old son is no longer with them. He was still in St. Louis in 1910 and, at age sixty-six, he was still working as a railroad conductor.

Then, on September 7, 1916, James Merrifield suffered a cerebral hemorrhage and died. He is buried at the Valhalla Cemetery in Bel-Nor, St. Louis County.

Merton, James Francis – 1871

Korean Expedition

James Merton was born in Cheshire, England in 1845. It is not known exactly when or why he emigrated to the United States but he was here, in his mid-twenties, and serving as a Carpenter and Landsman in the Navy when troubles began in Korea.

There were several factors that lead to the problems. One was the ruling isolationist dynasty. Another was a missing American merchant ship, and a third reason was an overly-aggressive diplomatic effort on the part of the Americans. The U.S. was asking for a treaty assuring aid for shipwrecked sailors, trade with Korea, and news of the missing merchant ship.

The American delegation was turned away with fire from Korean shore batteries which targeted two American warships. The American Admiral demanded an apology but received none. So, on June 10, 1871, 546 Navy Landsmen and

105 Marines landed, captured two fortresses, and killed over 200 Korean troops (known as the Tiger Hunters). Three Americans died. But Korea still refused to negotiate.

The American fleet wanted to steam up the Han River to the Korean Capital but Ganghwa Island held several forts that

blocked access to the river. To clear the way, the sailors and Marines were sent to attack and overcome the forts one after another until the way was clear. During the attack on one of these forts, Landsman Merton was shot and severely wounded. Details of his action were not given but his officers considered his actions to be worthy of the nation's highest honor. His Medal of Honor Citation tells us only:

"Landsman and member of Company D during the capture of the Korean forts, 9 and 10 June 1871, Merton was severely wounded in the arm while trying to force his way into the fort."

When Merton left the Navy, he went to Massachusetts where he married Mary E., who had also been born in England. They had three children, Charles, Ada, and Albert, then moved to St. Louis sometime after 1877. The Merton family made their home at 3946 Fair Avenue in St. Louis. This appears to be a rooming house with sleeping porches for the summer heat. It is directly across from the lake in Fairgrounds Park. James and Mary lived there for the rest of James' life. He died on January 9, 1922 and is buried in the Bellefontaine Cemetery.

Moore, Wilbur Fiske — Civil War

Wilbur Moore was born in Lebanon, Illinois on May 24, 1840 and lived there for his early years. When he was twenty-one, he left his farm and went to Summerfield, IL where, on August 13, 1862m he enlisted in the Union Army. His enlistment papers tell us that he was five feet, five inches tall with brown hair, gray eyes, and a dark complexion. He signed up for three years.

The 117th Illinois Volunteer Infantry served most of their three-year existence in Tennessee. They were transferred to Jefferson Barracks at one point and from there, they pursued Sterling Price around Missouri. In all, they seemed to have had a comparatively easy time during the war. They lost only eleven enlisted men killed or mortally wounded. However, 115 enlisted men and four officers died of disease.

From Jefferson Barracks they marched back to Tennessee and took part in the Battle of Nashville, December 15-16, 1864. In that struggle, the Confederates were entrenched on what was then called Compton's Hill. When Wilbur's unit charged the Confederates, he was far ahead of others in his regiment and led the way, capturing a Confederate battery's battle flag in the process. He was called to Washington, D.C. and stood before Secretary of War, Edwin M. Stanton to receive the Medal of Honor which was awarded in recognition of the courage displayed that day.

At the war's conclusion, Private Moore went to Springfield, IL where he mustered out on August 5, 1865. He returned to his boyhood home and married Emily Caroline Cuddy of that place. Then he did what so many seemed to have done at that time, they moved to Kansas City. It may be that Kansas City was considered to be the extreme west at that time. Kansas was new to the Union and Nebraska had not yet have sufficient population to join. Oklahoma was still a few decades away from becoming a state. The  railroads needed labor to complete and expand their lines and the cattle drives brought additional prosperity.

Whatever brought them, Wilbur, Emily, her two brothers, and their families all came to Kansas City. Wilbur and Emily lived at 4320 East 27th Street. Today that is a residential neighborhood at the corner of 27th and Kensington but it must have been a farm in 1865. Over the years, Wilbur bought, owned, and sold a great deal of real estate in the K.C. area.

Emily died in 1923 and the next year, Wilbur contracted pneumonia but there was no antibiotic treatment at that time. He died from that condition on December 9, 1924 and is buried with Emily at Forest Hill Cemetery in Kansas City.

O'Hare, Edward Henry – World War II

The father of our next hero was E.J. "Eddie" O'Hare, an outgoing, ambitious, and very bright man who lived in St. Louis and married a young St. Louis woman. They started their married life in an apartment in the Soulard District. That's where their son was born. Eddie was the picture of ambition. He ran his own business on the St. Louis waterfront, and attended college classes at St. Louis University. He worried about his son, Butch, who would often be laying around their home and reading. E.J. was afraid that Butch had a lazy streak. Because of that, he enrolled his boy in the Western Military Academy in Alton.

With all three of his children now busy with their schooling, Eddie began to grow his business. He first expanded from the St. Louis Levee to Chicago. Discovering that he loved to fly, he would sometimes "hitch" a ride between St. Louis and Chicago with a young airmail pilot named Charles Lindbergh. He even managed sometimes to let his son, Butch, ride along. Butch was allowed to take the plane's controls on at least one occasion.

Eddie passed the Missouri Bar Exam and joined a law firm in the city. Eventually he bought the family a wonderful new home in the Holly Hills neighborhood. It had a swimming pool and a skating rink! But at some point along the way he seems to have been recruited by the scar-faced Gangster, Al Capone for his talents as a "counselor and business manager," not for his criminal expertise. Be that as it may, E.J. was known to be the manager of dog racing tracks in Chicago, Miami, and Boston. In 1939, Eddie had gone temporarily to Chicago but Butch, who was born and raised in St. Louis was a new officer in the Navy and was being trained as an aviator at the Naval Air Station in Pensacola. Capone was serving his eighth year for income tax evasion. Chicago is where Eddie O'Hare was gunned down on the street with a shotgun.

I don't think that anyone doubts that Capone was responsible for the shooting but it did leave a mystery which has never been truly solved. One story says that Eddie understood that Capone was involved in illegal activities and he, Eddie O'Hare, wanted out. This account says that he went to the U.S. Treasury officials and offered to give the evidence that was needed to convict the gangster. The family claims that he was trying to do the right thing and make up for his previous poor judgment.

Another, more interesting version, says that the father understood that he was in danger and would never really be out. He wanted his son to make a life away from the Capone organization. This account tells that the father made a bargain with the Treasury Department and gave them evidence needed to convict Capone in exchange for his son's acceptance into officer training at Annapolis. However, it transpired, the father was gunned down, Capone was still in prison, and young Butch was finishing his flight training with the Navy.

During his childhood Butch had gone many times with his family to camping spots on the Gasconade and Meramec Rivers and while there he would shoot his .22 at tin cans as they floated by. Hitting those moving targets started his skill as a marksman and would serve him well as a fighter pilot. But before the war ever got started Butch asked Rita Wooster, a nurse at Deaconess Hospital, to marry him and a few weeks later they wed. Then he was sent back into service flying off the carrier, USS Saratoga, which was undergoing maintenance at the time.

The Saratoga was still in port when the Japanese attacked Pearl Harbor so she steamed for Pearl Harbor the next day. Soon Butch's squadron was transferred to duty aboard the USS Lexington. From that ship he saw his first combat in the skies north of Australia. He and his wingman spotted a group of Japanese dive bombers headed for the Lexington. The two American pilots fired test shots and found that all four of the wingman's machine

guns had jammed. As Butch attacked alone, anti-aircraft fire was coming from the carrier group but Butch flew right through it and continued his assault on the bombers. The sailors of the carrier group watched as Butch downed five Japanese planes in less than four minutes! That made him the Navy's first "Ace" in the Pacific and it earned him the Medal of Honor.

The war was going badly for America and the country needed a hero. The handsome young pilot from the Heartland was just the person to fill that role. Within a few days Butch and Rita were calling on the President at 1600 Pennsylvania Avenue. By August of '43 Butch was back in Hawaii and was promoted to Air-Group Commander. He was now in charge of three squadrons of the new Hellcat fighters. This fighter group was ordered to join aboard the USS Enterprise which was headed for the Gilbert Islands.

Anyone interested in naval aviation owe it to themselves to read about the night-fighting flights that O'Hare improvised to protect our WW II carriers. The concept was both innovative and effective. I won't bore you with all of the details of Butch O'Hare's military career. You can always look that up if you choose.

We do need to recognize that he was active in the hectic push through the Pacific toward total victory. I do want to record that he was flying the Navy's new Hellcat fighter when he was shot down on November 26, 1943 while defending his aircraft carrier from attack. He was only twenty-nine. His plane went down near the Gilbert Islands and his body could not be recovered.

You can read in many places about the pride Chicago feels toward their native son, Butch O'Hare. That pride is why they named the Airport in his honor. After all, he moved there as a teenager – right? The truth of the matter is that Butch had visited Chicago on a few occasions with his father but he didn't live there even one day of his life. He grew up in the Soulard Neighborhood above a grocery store and in the pleasant Holly Hills neighborhood of South St. Louis. He married a St. Louis girl and they were stationed at various naval bases but Butch was one of ours – a somewhat forgotten (or at least misplaced) hero from Missouri.

Opel, John Nicholas – Civil War

Have you been to Opel, Missouri? Well, not in this lifetime. It ceased to exist back at the turn of the last century. But it was a prosperous little farming community with a store and a post office catering to the needs of the farm families settled there on that fertile plain. It was right between Cora, Owasco, and Paw Paw, near Winnigan. But probably only some of the folks, even in Sullivan County, realize that it was named for a Medal of Honor recipient.

Johann Nikolaus Opel was born July 30, 1843 in Hoflas, Nűrnberger Land, Bayern. (now Bavaria, Germany) He came with his parents, Johann Wolfgang and Anna Kay Fisher Opel, to America and went first to Indiana but eventually settled on the rich soil of Sullivan County,

Missouri. He was the youngest of nine children and was twelve years old when he came to America.

By the time he entered the Army, he had anglicized his name and was known as John. John did enter the Army at the beginning of the Civil War and served throughout. He is best remembered though for his actions on May 5, 1864. At that time Private Opel was in the Wilderness Campaign in Virginia. On the first day of battle, he captured the regimental flag of the 50th Virginia Infantry (C.S.A.). Capturing an enemy battle flag was considered a noteworthy goal and doing so earned John the Medal of Honor.

His unit marched onward and took part in the battle of Port Republic on June 8, 1863. In that fight, John took a serious wound to his right arm. Because of his wound, he lost much of the use of that arm. A grateful nation gave him a disability pension when his enlistment was up. He received $2.00 per month.

At war's end, John came back to Missouri and settled in Sullivan County in 1870. That land on which he settled would remain his home for the rest of his life, fifty-five years. He was twenty-four (1867) when he married Phebe Ann Sloan and they had six children. The Postal Service needed a post office and a post master in the area where John lived so he applied and was named the Post Master for the community. The actual post office was in his farmhouse and people would naturally say that they were going to the Opel place for their mail. They told everyone to send mail to them at the Opel Post Office. So, until 1905, there was an official community that carried the name of the most famous person in the area, John Opel. He was also one of the most prosperous citizens with 220 acres under cultivation.

Private John N. Opel was visiting in Cora, Missouri when he died on February 21, 1905. He and Phebe are buried at the Mount Zion Cemetery at the Mount Zion Methodist Episcopal Church in Sullivan County.

Pearsall, Platt – Civil War

Read the section on the Missouri Men of Forlorn Hope, page 66 to read more about Henry Platt Pearsall.

Peden, Forrest E. – World War II

A successful military campaign may call for all sorts of sacrifices. Forrest Peden did what someone needed to do but few would have the courage for it. His buddies called him "Frosty" and he was cool and deliberate about what he did in France in 1945.

He was just a "regular kid" growing up. He was born October 3, 1913 in St. Joseph. His grandparents had been the first in the family to live in St. Joseph. Then they spelled the

family name as "Paden." But Forrest's father, Joseph, dropped the "a" and doubled down on the "e" to give the present spelling. Joseph married Maude Kerns from there in Buchannan County. Forrest lived in St. Joseph during his early years but the family moved just across the river to Wathena, Kansas before he joined the Army. His twin brothers also joined the Army and one of them died in World War II.

February 3, 1945 found Technician 5th Grade, Frosty Peder with the Third Infantry Division near Biesheim, France. He was a forward artillery observer and advancing with about 45 men when the group was ambushed. They soon realized that they were badly outnumbered. They were being hit with artillery, mortar, machinegun, and small-arms fire when they spotted a ditch and ran for safety. But the enemy was already in the ditch so, instead of jumping into safety, they jumped into hand-to-hand combat.

Two men quickly fell wounded and Peden rushed to them and began rendering first aid. At that moment he knew they needed help but the radios were inoperative. He had to do something to bring help. So he ran the gauntlet for over a half-mile to the Batallion Command Post. When he arrived, his jacket had several bullet holes.

Peden was able to get two light tanks to go to the aid of his unit. He exposed himself to great danger by riding atop one of the tanks and guiding it to the exact spot where his unit was pinned down. His Medal of Honor Citation tells us:

> *"Bullets and shell fragments ricocheting from its steel armor within inches of the completely exposed rider, until it reached the ditch. As it was about to go into action it was turned into a flaming pyre by a direct hit which killed Technician Peden."*

The tank sat there burning but it burned so brightly that it helped the other reinforcements find the ambushed Americans. It's light even helped the Americans to see their attackers better and to engage them more effectively.

One historian later wrote, "Peden's actions were responsible for thwarting a German ambush, enabling the 7th infantry to successfully carry out its mission to capture Biesheim—a small thing, perhaps, in the bigger picture of the war, but more importantly, his actions saved the lives of many of his comrades."

Sad to say, Frosty Peden's twin brothers also had tough going in that war. One was killed in Italy and the other wounded by the same artillery shell. Another casualty was the little daughter, Marcia, that Frosty left behind. Almost all she remembered of her father was his climbing aboard the train on the day he shipped out.

A U.S. Army website declared that Peden, "was a valiant soldier whose deeds seem to have drifted into that obscurity,"

Another observer wants us to remember that, "Many lives were saved thanks to Peden's selfless heroism."

Pentzer, Patrick Henry — Civil War

The baby boy who would be known as Henry Pentzer was born on September 24, 1838 in Marion County, Missouri. He was the oldest of the six children of Valentine Pentzer and his wife, Ann. Valentine was a teacher at Marion College and the founder and Minister for the Rattan's Prairie Church and later he preached at the Dry Point Church across the river in Illinois. We could find nothing about his early years but the wartime letters from his mother indicate that Henry was expected to assume the "big brother" role and protect his younger brother, Thomas, who was serving with him.

When the war began between the North and South, Henry and Thomas crossed the river to Macoupin County, Illinois and joined the 97th Illinois Volunteer Infantry. He was appointed as Captain and the Commander of Company C. Our interest in Captain Pentzer comes from his actions at Fort Blakely, Alabama on April 9, 1865.

On that momentous day, the Union forces were attacking entrenched Confederate forces when Captain Pentzer led a charge and breached the enemy defenses. He took a Confederate General as a prisoner and captured his headquarters flag. That was the act which earned him the Medal of Honor but he had several other noteworthy experiences before war's end.

He was sent from place to place as the circumstances dictated. We know that he and Thomas spent a good deal of time running a camp for prisoners of war which was located at New Orleans. At one time, a train carrying both Henry and Thomas wrecked but the brothers survived without serious injury. Another day, Captain Pentzer captured some Rebel soldiers and took them out to show where "land torpedoes" had been planted. These must have been land mines.

Eventually the war ended and Henry returned to his Missouri home. He married Mary F. Adams and they had two children. They lived in a farming community called Philadelphia in Marion County. It had been given its name by Henry's father, Valentine, in honor of his own birthplace. It lies between Palmyra and Shelbyville.

Henry died at Philadelphia, Missouri on October 16, 1901. He is buried in the National Cemetery in Springfield, Missouri. Mary received a $20/month widow's benefit because of Henry's service and outlived him by just a few years.

Pesch, Joseph M. – Civil War

Read the section on the Men of The *J.W. Cheeseman*, page 107, to read more about Joseph M. Pesch.

Phoenix, Edwin – Indian Wars

The Red River War was a military campaign of the US Army in 1874 against the Kiowa, Southern Cheyenne, Comanche, and the Arapaho nations. Its purpose was to forcibly relocate them to reservations in the Indian Territory. (Oklahoma) The Army sent several columns crisscrossing the Texas Panhandle trying to locate then harass or capture the highly mobile Native bands. The ultimate goal being submission and removal.

By the end of 1874 only a few tribes had the strength or resources needed to hold out against the Cavalry. One of the tribes, the Southern Cheyenne still had the power to resist and, on September 26, 1874, were camped in five groups at Canyon Blanco, a tributary of the Red River. After locating them, Colonel R.S. Mackenzie sent elements of his 4th US Cavalry to the attack. The fight lasted two days and there are many somewhat conflicting accounts of what transpired. In this writer's opinion, the best account came from a civilian merchant who accompanied the Fourth that day. In the _New North West_ newspaper, Deer Lodge, Montana, Jerry Fahey tells us:

> _"About 3 ½ o'clock Sunday morning…we took the trail again; traveled about 10 miles before finding water; cooked breakfast by fire the Indians had left. After a slim breakfast, we took the trail again, traveled fully 20 miles farther when Sanders_

(the other citizen) and myself discovered a very fine bay horse off to one side. Sanders remarked that the Indians could not be very far off, because they never would have left so fine an animal behind them."

"First Serg't Phoenix, who was ahead was observed motioning with his hand, and a halt was ordered. The Indians were camped just ahead... Phoenix, as he rolled up his sleeves, remarked to the men (we were very thirsty) 'Boys, we'll have water in 20 minutes; we've got to have it.'"

"We then crept towards the camp gathering behind a big log and some brush, about 400 yards from the river. Some of the men were a little way behind, when suddenly an Indian, mounted on the fine bay horse mentioned above, came galloping down the gulch, whooping and halloaing for Lord's sake. Some of the men fired on him killing his horse but I think he got away."

"Most of the boys, however, turned loose on the camp, and then over the log we jumped and broke for them, running over an open space straight for the camp, yelling and hooping at the top of our voices. The firing reminded me of a pack of firecrackers. It was wonderful how rapidly the boys loaded and fired."

"The Indians had only two or three rods to run to the brush and we were ordered to take to the trees. Sergeant Phoenix was the only man who went directly into the hostile camp, and I never expected to see him come out alive. He cut the stock loose, mounted on a fine stallion, and drove the herd in our direction. His horse shot under him, but he escaped without a scratch. While he was in the camp the boys cracked away at every moving thing and probably saved his life by the rapidity and precision of their firing."

"For two hours the battle raged, and then the firing ceased until sundown, when four or five Indians came down and tried to retake the horses. The liveliest kind of firing took place for a few moments, and the supposition is that three of the party will never need horses again. One Indian was heard to shout over the camp soon after, but that was the last we heard of them."

Being without horses in that time and place meant being without transportation to food and especially water. In many ways, people without horses were almost defenseless against mounted opponents. They were vital to life. Just as the Cheyenne tried to get the horses away from the Cavalry, Sergeant Phoenix's capturing of the Native's horses, was a major tactical victory. It should also be noted that the number of horses captured and driven off by the Sergeant's daring actions totaled about 1,400 animals. Only four Native warriors were killed but the horses determined the true outcome and importance of the battle.

While they were in camp that evening, there was a pleasant surprise. A mule which had belonged to the merchant, Fahey, came walking into camp and, with his cargo of cooking pots, beans, coffee, rice, sugar, raw beef, and fresh fish. This provided the men with a pleasant break from their normal camp situation. It was reported that their Lieutenant made them move almost without stopping and then only for a lunch of some bread cooked on a stick over a small fire.

Compared to other military operations, the scale of this one was pretty small. But this skirmish was one of the final and decisive engagements bringing the campaign nearer to its end. The war marked the end of the free-roaming nomadic lifestyle of the populations on the Southern Great Plains.

As with most people who chose the military as a career, Edwin Phoenix traveled from post to post. The boy from St. Louis, now an older man, eventually arrived in California. He died there in Los Angeles on September 5, 1932 and is buried in the Los Angeles National Cemetery.

Phillips, George – World War II

The young Marine Reserve Private known as "Junior" was born on July 14, 1926 in Rich Hill, Missouri. When he was only three years old, his parents both died and he was sent across the state to live with his aunt and uncle, Lillian and James O'Brien, in Labadie, Missouri. His three brothers and sisters all went to live with various aunts and uncles in different locales.

Junior's new home of Labadie is a historic little town in Franklin County and today it's home to nice restaurants, antique shops, and a very pleasant place. In the 1930s, however, it was definitely off the beaten path. Instead of "Junior" his new step-brother and his step-sister seem to have called him "Junie." The picture below shows that officially he remained George Phillips.

In this 1931 photo, George is in the second row, second from the left wearing dark bib overalls.

George attended church services and Sunday School at the local Methodist Church with his family. A friend, Emmett Becker remembered Junior feeling lucky because he lived just down the hill from the school and didn't have to walk too far. He also remembered Junior enjoying "corncob wars" as the boys threw the cobs at each other.

His sister, Edna Dutton remembered him as quiet and shy. She said that he loved Christmas and all the festivities that go along with it. His ambition was to play baseball in the big leagues and he practiced a lot. His school was small and, when he graduated from eighth grade, there were only three graduates. He earned a certificate for perfect attendance.

Junior worked helping several area farmers and then landed a steady job as a painter on the Shell Oil Company's pipeline that ran near Labadie. Then, still a young man, Junior won a coveted job on the railroad. He worked on a "section gang" keeping the track maintained. A section hand worked hard but got paid well and was almost always pretty close to home. A job like that during the years of the Great Depression was a thing to be treasured.

When World War II began, two of his step-brothers joined the Army and Junior gave a lot of thought to what he should do. He made up his mind that he definitely wanted to be a Marine. So, he went to Jefferson City to obtain a copy of his birth certificate and, on April 26, 1944, Seventeen-year-old George Phillips became a Marine.

Basic Training at Camp Pendleton was soon over and he got a short furlough. He came home in uniform to see his friends and family. They might have worried that it would be there last time to see him. They would have been right.

Junior was attached to the 5th Marine Division as a replacement in the assault on Iwo Jima. He and others listed as replacements were to help other groups come ashore and wait their turn to replace other men who had been killed or injured. Another young man in the unit described coming ashore as the ships fired shells into the island and the Japanese returned the fire. Most of the Japanese artillery seemed to be located on the volcanic mountain, Suribachi.

Another replacement described landing materials and munitions on a dead run. When night fell, they carried stretchers to waiting LSMs (Landing Ship Mediums) to carry the wounded to hospital ships – until the hospital ships were full and could accept no more. He said that, while they worked on the beach, artillery shells, mortar shells, and machine gun fire poured down on them from Suribachi.

Finally, they began to send in the "green kids" as replacements. Many were killed or wounded before anyone had a chance to learn their names. Junior was sent to Company F of the 28th Marines. Company F was sent on a flanking movement around the entrenched guns that were playing havoc with the Marines. That night brought a surprise attack but Company F managed to kill twenty-seven of the attackers and another thirty shortly afterward. The fighting continued like this day after day.

Then During the night of March 14, 1945, Junior was standing guard while other exhausted Marines were trying to get some rest. Suddenly, a Japanese soldier appeared and lobbed a hand grenade among the group of Marines. Without hesitating, Junior threw himself on the grenade in order to absorb the full impact of the explosion and thereby save his comrades. George was killed instantly. It was this entirely selfless act that earned George "Junior" Phillips his country's highest honor.

Missouri's 18-year-old hero was posthumously awarded the Medal of Honor and was buried in a military grave on the island of Iwo Jima. But, in 1948, his body was reinterred and now rests in the Cemetery at his Bethel Methodist Church in Labadie.

His Medal of Honor Citation tells us:

"For conspicuous gallantry and intrepidity at the risk of his life above and beyond the call of duty while serving with the Second Battalion, Twenty-Eighth Marines, Fifth Marine Division, in action against Japanese forces during the seizure of Iwo Jima in the Volcano Islands, on 14 March 1945. Standing fox-hole watch while other members of his squad rested after a night of bitter hand grenade fighting against infiltrating Japanese troops, Private Phillips was the only member of his unit alerted when an enemy hand grenade was tossed into their midst. Instantly shouting a warning, he unhesitatingly threw himself on the deadly missile, absorbing the shattering violence of the exploding charge in his own body and protecting his comrades from serious injury.

Stout-hearted and indomitable, Private Phillips willingly yielded his own life that his fellow Marines might carry on the relentless battle against a fanatic enemy and his superb valor and unfaltering spirit of self-sacrifice in the face of certain death reflect the highest credit upon himself and upon the United States Naval Service. He gallantly gave his life for his country."

205

Porter, Ambrose M. – Civil War

Ambrose Porter was born in Maryland on February 2, 1839 as the tenth child in a family of eleven children. His parents were Henry and Lydia (Majors) Porter. When he was five years old, the family moved to a farm in Ohio and when he was eight, his father died and his mother moved into the nearby town. At seventeen he began to learn the trade of a carpenter.

In 1858 he left home and moved to Atchison County, Missouri where he started a farm and practiced his carpentry. On October 14, 1861 he enlisted for a six-month hitch in the Union Army. Serving in various Missouri Infantry and Cavalry units, he worked his way up through the ranks and was soon a Commissary Sergeant. Eventually he held the rank of Lieutenant.

On August 7, 1864, Ambrose was serving as Commissary Sergeant of Company D, 12th Missouri Volunteer Infantry. They were engaging the enemy on the Tallahatchie River in Mississippi. The Confederates had established a strong defensible position on one bank of the river and the Missouri Infantry couldn't cross the river to dislodge them. There was a ferry boat but the Rebels had it on their side and under their control.

That was the situation when Ambrose Porter and three other volunteers swam across the river under heavy fire and seized the ferry. Somehow, they were able to dodge enough bullets to bring the boat back to the Union-controlled side of the river. The 12th Missouri was then able to use the ferry to take enough troops across the river and dislodge their enemy from their strong position. It was his bravery on that day which earned him the Medal of Honor.

At war's end, Ambrose returned to Atchison County and took a position as Station Agent for the Kansas City, St. Joseph, & Corn Belt Rail Road Company in Phelps City, Missouri. He was a well-respected citizen who served as Justice of the Peace of Templeton Township and a member of the Town Board for Phelps City. He owned a good deal of real estate including the two-story Dewey Hotel.

In October of 1867 he went to Memphis, Tennessee and married Mary A. Worthington of that city. In 1892, they had one daughter, Cleta, who looked after her father when Mary died in 1901. Ambrose was back at home in Atchison County where records list him only as "retired." Then, after he had been ailing with "LaGrippe" (influenza) for about two weeks, he died suddenly of a heart attack on January 21, 1916. He was a few days short of his 77th birthday. He is buried in the Elmwood Cemetery in Rockport.

Quick, John Henry – Spanish-American War

John Henry Quick is used as an example for young Marine recruits. He is about the best role model that the marines could find for their training manual. He served in the Corps for twenty-six years and participated in every campaign the Marines were involved in during that time. He won several

awards for valor which we will discuss later. Sergeant Major Quick fought in the West Indies Campaign, the Spanish-American War, the Philippine-American War, the Cuban Campaign, the Battle of Vera Cruz, and World War I.

He was born on June 20, 1870 in Charleston, West Virginia but, at age twenty-two, he was in Philadelphia where he enlisted in the

Marine Corps. He was already a seasoned veteran when the Marines were sent into action in the Spanish-American War. In July, 1898, the Spanish forces were holding an important water supply in Cuzco, Cuba. On the 14th, two companies of Marines were sent to capture that well. As they advanced on the well, they came under attack.

The USS Dolphin was sitting in Guantanamo Bay in support of the mission. The Marines signaled the Dolphin to provide supporting gunfire but the signal was misinterpreted and the Marines came under "friendly fire" from the ship's guns.

Sergeant Quick made himself visible to the ship's crew and signaled for a cease-fire. The flag he was using was not visible enough and the ship's gunners didn't understand. So he climbed to the top of a nearby hill. He made himself visible to the ship but also to the enemy and he came under heavy rifle fire. Quick calmly turned his back on the enemy and continued to signal letter by letter sending Morse code until he completed the message. Then he picked up his rifle and rejoined the fight.

A war correspondent, Stephen Crane, witnessed the event and wrote:

> *"I watched his face, and it was as grave and serene as a man writing in his own library . . . I saw Quick betray only one sign of emotion. As he swung his clumsy flag back and forth, an end of it once caught on a cactus pillar. He looked annoyed."*

He wrote further, *"He was the very embodiment of tranquility in occupation."*

"Stand Marines. He served on Samar," became a salute among Marines honoring the men who made a heroic march across the island of Samar during the Philippine Insurrection. John Quick is credited with inspiring the other Marines to continue and complete their ordeal.

Sergeant Major Quick was involved in many important campaigns including the Battle at Belleau Wood (World War I) where the American Marines taught an Old World army what the Marines were all about. This is where they earned the name, "Devil Dogs." Quick himself earned a Navy Cross and a Distinguished Service Cross in that campaign.

Sergeant Major Quick retired from the Marine Corps on November 20, 1918 and married Edith Yoos. They chose to live in her home town of St. Louis. Sadly, he didn't have long to enjoy his new life. He died in St. Louis, Mo., September 10, 1922. He was forty-eight years old. John and Edith are both buried in the Memorial Park Cemetery in Jennings.

Too often, heroism is forgotten soon after the medal arrives. But that was not the case with this Marine. The funeral procession from his church to the cemetery included two detachments from the Missouri National Guard, the Veterans of Foreign Wars, the Grand Army of the Republic, the Marine Corps Club, various American Legion Posts, and the Knights of Pythias. The St. Louis Police Department provided a platoon of mounted policemen (all former servicemen), and a marching band from the Naval Reserve.

At graveside, the Marines had a bugler play taps and an honor guard of eight rifles for a salute. When the casket, resting on an artillery caisson, reached the grave, two airplanes flew over and released flowers.

Honorary pallbearers included Mayor Kiel, Col. John Parker, Gen. E.J. Spencer, and Thomas Skinker, whose family would have a Medal of Honor winner in just a few years. Other honorary pallbearers were William Danforth, Thomas Watts, and Governor David R. Francis who was known as the Father of the University of Missouri and the Chairman of the 1904 St. Louis World's Fair.

This rivaled the funerals that St. Louis provided for General William T. Sherman and for the heroic fireman, Phelim O'Toole. It should be an example to other communities as they recognize their own.

Note:

In addition to the medals earned by Sergeant Major Quick, the Navy named a destroyer, the USS Quick in his honor. It earned four battle stars during World War II. There was also a Liberty Ship named the SS John H. Quick in his memory.

Riordan, Paul F. — World War II

Paul F. Riordan was born on Nov. 8, 1920, one of eight children of bookkeeper, Herbert F. and Orpha J. Riordan. They lived at 4045 Walnut Street in Kansas City's south side about fifteen blocks south of Hallmark's Crown Center. He attended school at the Visitation Parochial School and as a young man, he worked as a shipping clerk at the Montgomery Ward headquarters not far from his house.

By the time Paul enlisted in May, 1940, two of his older brothers were already in service. One was a Sergeant in the Army and another was a Naval Aviation Cadet. In May, 1942 he sailed with the 34th Infantry Division, U.S. Army which was the first American division deployed to Europe in World War II. Their job was to attack "the soft underbelly of Europe" which, of course turned out not to be so soft.

On 24 January 1944, during the First Battle of Monte Cassino in Italy, they

pushed across the Gari River into the hills and attacked the rear of Monastery Hill, which dominated the town of Monte Cassino. The performance of the 34th Infantry Division in the mountains has been called one of the finest feats of arms carried out by any soldiers during the war. Eventually, it took the combined force of five Allied infantry divisions to finish what the 34th nearly accomplished on its own.

Riordan's Medal of Honor Citation detailed his actions:

"For conspicuous gallantry and intrepidity above and beyond the call of duty."

"In the attack on the approaches to the city of Cassino on February 3, 1944, 2d Lt. Riordan led 1 of the assault platoons. Attacking Hill 175, his command was pinned down by enemy machinegun fire from the hill and from a pillbox about 45 yards to the right of the hill. In the face of intense fire, 2d Lt. Riordan moved out in full view of the enemy gunners to reach a position from where he could throw a hand grenade into the pillbox. Then, getting to his knees, he hurled the grenade approximately 45 yards, scoring a direct hit. The grenade killed 1 and wounded the other 2 Germans in the nest and silenced the gun. Another soldier then cleaned out the enemy pillboxes on the hill itself, and the company took its objective."

"Continuing the assault into Cassino itself on February 8, 1944, 2d Lt. Riordan and his platoon were given the mission of taking the city jail house, one of the enemy's several strongpoints. Again 2d Lt. Riordan took the lead and managed to get through the ring of enemy fire covering the approaches and reached the building. His platoon, however, could not get through the intense fire and was cut off. 2d Lt. Riordan, aware that his men were unable to follow, determined to carry on single-handed, but the

> *numerically superior enemy force was too much for him to overcome, and he was killed by enemy small-arms fire after disposing of at least 2 of the defenders."*

> *"2d Lt. Riordan's bravery and extraordinary heroism in the face of almost certain death were an inspiration to his men and exemplify the highest traditions of the U.S. Armed Forces."*

The Riordan family was notified on February 8th that their son was missing in action and four days later they were informed of Paul's heroic death.

During his time in the Army, he also received the Purple Heart, the American Defense Service Medal, the World War II Victory Medal, the American Campaign Medal (Europe/African/Middle Eastern Campaign), and the French Croix de Guerre, WW II.

The Medal of Honor was presented to Paul's parents on September 11, 1944 at their home in Kansas City where about thirty friends and relatives attended the ceremony. Included in that number were Mr. and Mrs. Elmer Specker from Odessa, Missouri. Their son, Sergeant Joseph Specker had, just a few weeks earlier been awarded his own Medal of Honor posthumously for actions during his service in Italy. Riordan and Specker were both twenty-three-years old when they died in action. You can read about Joe Specker's life in the following pages.

Second Lieutenant Riordan was originally buried in the American Battlefield Memorial Cemetery in Italy but his family requested that the body be brought home and he rests today with other family members in the Mount Olivet Cemetery in Raytown.

Ryan, David – Frontier Indian Campaigns

David Ryan was born in 1836 in County Kilkenny, Ireland. He came to the United States and, like so many other Irishmen, joined the Army. He was a forty-year-old Private when he found himself with the 5th U.S. Infantry (mounted) in the Northern Plains. The Sioux and Cheyenne had won a major victory at the Little Bighorn and the Army was looking for retribution.

They pursued a large number of Sioux across an area roughly from the Black Hills to the Yellowstone River and finally, the Natives asked to meet with Colonel Miles and they would be represented by the Hunkpapa Chief, Sitting Bull. The two met at Cedar Creek, Montana Territory with about 300 Native warriors on one side of the leaders and almost 400 soldiers on the other side. The talks went badly and a running battle covering about forty-two miles ensued.

On October 27, 1876, over four hundred lodges (with about 2,000 men, women, and children) surrendered and returned to their reservations. Sitting Bull and a smaller number of his followers continued northward hoping to find refuge in Canada.

It was during the running battle described above that Private Ryan was recognized for gallantry. There is really no description of just what he did but his Medal of Honor Citation tells us it was presented by the United States Army, *"for gallantry in engagements at Cedar Creek, Montana and other campaigns during the period 21 October 1876 to 8 January 1877, while serving with Company G, 5th U.S. Infantry."*

His presentation ceremony was at a parade in the cantonment at the confluence of the Yellowstone and the

Tongue Rivers in Montana. General William T. Sherman presented the medal.

Little is known about David Ryan after that date. We do know that he eventually earned his Sergeant's stripes and that he was transferred back to Jefferson Barracks in St. Louis. In that city he would have found a very large Irish community and that may be why he decided to retire there.

Sergeant David Ryan died in St. Louis on September 8, 1896. He is buried at the Jefferson Barracks National Cemetery.

Schubert, Martin – Civil War

Martin Schubert was still another of our Missouri Medal of Honor recipients who was born in Germany. That took place on June 29, 1838. He probably came into the U.S. through an East Coast port rather than New Orleans as many German-Missourians did. He was in his mid-twenties when he enlisted with an infantry unit, the 26th New York, and was involved in the Battle of Antietam, where he was seriously wounded. He was granted a furlough, (some records say a medical discharge) but instead, he rejoined his unit on its way to Fredericksburg.

Schubert described his situation there at Frederiksberg. *"My old wound, not yet healed, still gave me considerable trouble. I went into the battle with the regiment, however, against the protests of my colonel and captain, who insisted that I should use the furlough. I thought the Government needed me on the battlefield rather than at home."*

He carried the regimental colors into the battle and caught another bullet in his left side. *"I still carry the bullet,"* he wrote years later.

One account tells that Maj. Gen. Ambrose Burnside discovered that Schubert had gone into battle instead of on furlough, and promised him a Medal of Honor on the spot.

Another report tells us, "As their colors fell to the earth, a German immigrant sprang forward. Martin Schubert should not have been on the battlefield at Fredericksburg. Schubert was sickly and had just received a medical discharge from the army. Rather than abandon his comrades and flag in their time of need, though, Schubert had stayed to fight. He scooped up the flag and, rather than just stand his ground, he strode forward, urging his unit to follow. Moments later, Schubert was felled by a bullet—but another immigrant stepped in to take up the colors and the advance. Joseph Keene, a former Englishman, took the flag from Schubert and helped to keep the advance going."

Before retiring from the Army, Schubert achieved the rank of First Lieutenant. He mustered out at Jefferson Barracks and decided to remain in St. Louis, where he lived for the rest of his life.

Little is known about him during his years in retirement. We know that he married "Philli" Zimmerman and they raised three children. He worked as a butcher in the city. He must have appreciated the large German community that thrived in St. Louis. That may be why he stayed. At any rate, St. Louis was the only American city where he had a permanent home. He and Jill made their home at 1959 Garth Ave. in what we now call the Baden Neighborhood. In those days it was known as Germantown. In 1902 his Army pension was increased from $17 to $20 per month. When he was about 65, he began having troubles with bronchial asthma. Then, after eight years of treatment, it got the best of him and he died on April 25, 1912, just short of his 74th birthday. Lieutenant Schubert is buried in the National Cemetery at Jefferson Barracks.

Sisler,
George Kenton –
Vietnam

Ken Sisler was born (September 19, 1937) and grew up in Dexter, Missouri. He and one sister were the only siblings in the family. A childhood friend, and now a Dexter attorney, John W. Ringer, said Ken, "always had a spring in his step and he was easily embarrassed." He said, "I used to call out, "Hey George!" and he'd turn red. He never liked 'George,' Ringer said.

Ringer reports that Sisler went to Southeast Missouri State University and Arkansas State University to get his teaching degree. But before he started his teaching career, he took a job as a smoke jumper before entering the Army.

He served in the Army National Guard and then the Army Reserves from 1956 to 1962. In 1964, he completed the Bachelor's Degree that he had been working on. At that point he enlisted in the Regular Army and qualified for Officer Candidate School. He was commissioned a 2nd Lieutenant on June 22, 1965.

Soon promoted to 1st Lieutenant, Sisler was attached to Headquarters Company, 5th Special Forces Group (Airborne),

First Special Forces, Vietnam. His duties were as the Assistant Intelligence Officer.

On February 7, 1967, the platoon under his leadership had a veteran Green Beret (Sisler) leading them. They were deep in enemy territory when they were attacked on three sides. Sisler rallied his men, deployed them to a better defensive position and called in air strikes. Then he moved among his men offering encouragement.

He learned that two of his men were wounded and would be unable to pull back, so he charged from his position through intense gunfire to assist the wounded men. Carrying one of the wounded men to safety, he came under even heavier fire so he put the man down, killed three onrushing enemy, and knocked out a machine gun with a hand grenade. Then, just as he got his man back within the friendly perimeter, the enemy attacked his left flank with a superior force.

Understanding that his platoon was about to be overrun,

he picked up some grenades and charged single-handedly firing his rifle and throwing grenades. He was mortally wounded in that moment but his action broke up the assault and forced the enemy to begin a withdrawal. He saved the lives of a number of his men.

For his exemplary service in Vietnam, the selfless and courageous young man from Dexter earned the Bronze Star, the Purple Heart, the Medal of Honor, and several other major decorations.

Following his death, he was inducted into the Military Intelligence Corps Hall of Fame and the Intelligence Center named Sisler Hall on Fort Huachuca in his honor. In 1998 the Navy commissioned the USNS Sisler a large roll-on-roll-off vessel.

Ken Sisler is buried in the Dexter Cemetery in his home town. Recently the community erected a large bronze statue of him at the cemetery. Then an anonymous donor gave a large plaque which was made for the base of the statue. Ken's sister, Becky, said he would be embarrassed by the plaque and memorial statue. Then she added, "But he'd also be thrilled."

She said that an especially touching moment came when one of the younger members of the Sisler family climbed a ladder to place the Medal of Honor around the statue's neck.

Ken's widow, Jane said the Medal had never been around anyone's neck. She said, "You cannot put on the Medal of Honor unless you have earned it." George Kenton Sisler definitely earned it!

Skinker, Alexander Rives – World War I

Alexander Rives Skinker born the fifth child of six children in a wealthy and influential family. His grandfather had come to St. Louis and became a powerful and financially successful attorney. The grandfather, Thomas Skinker, is best remembered for his eloquent letter proposing the creation of Forest Park in St. Louis. The existence of this park created a place to build and host the World's Fair in 1904.

Residents of St. Louis will recognize that the entire western side of Forest Park is bounded by Skinker Boulevard, named for our hero's family. Skinker Boulevard is also the eastern boundary of Washington University. Alexander Skinker graduated from Smith academy and then from Washington University. One biographer described him as, "a model son, brother and husband, genial, kind, honorable, unselfish, energetic, judicious, temperate, and sure of himself, a Christian gentleman and a member of the Protestant Episcopal Church."

In 1903, while still in college, he enlisted in Battery A, St. Louis Light Artillery. Skinker graduated in 1905 and immediately took a position with the Long Distance Bell Telephone Company.

In 1916, he heard a speaker telling of the strong possibility of war with either Mexico or Germany and possibly both. The speaker said that the United States was woefully lacking in officers and he urged his audience to join in forming

a Officers' Training Corps. Aleck, as he had come to be known, along with six other young men accepted the offer and started a training corps. In a short time, there were two hundred and fifty men participating. Two hundred of these subsequently entered into military service when World War I began. They formed the Missouri National Guard.

In 1916, they were sent to the Mexican border. Aleck was promoted shortly after to Captain. They were back in St. Louis on March, 1917 when the company was called to guard the bridges across the Mississippi and Missouri, the City Water Works, the lead mines and smelters in the Mineral Area, and

223

the munitions factories in St. Louis. It was feared that German sympathizers might attack those places.

On August 11, 1917, Captain Skinker married Miss Caroline Rulon-Miller of Philadelphia. But he was sent almost immediately to Fort Sill, Oklahoma where two Missouri regiments were merged forming the One Hundred and Thirty-Eighth United States Infantry. Skinker was retained as Captain of Company I.

In April, 1918, the regiment was sent to Camp Mills, New York, and one week later, they boarded a ship for Europe. After a few days in England, they crossed into France. In August his regiment was marching to Bar-le-duc. They moved through the forested countryside mostly by night to avoid German airplanes. The attack on Argonne began on September 26 and Captain Skinker's unit was in front. They were attacking what has come to be known as the Hindenburg Line.

On that first day of the battle, Captain Skinker took two men with him and ordered the others to stay under cover. He went ahead to get the lay of the land and possibly spot the machine gun nest that was holding up their attack. Suddenly, they came under heavy machine gun fire and Captain Skinker was killed.

In an after-action report, the acting Regimental Commander wrote, "Captain Skinker, in his local area, not desiring to expose more men than were necessary, required his men to take cover, and personally set out with an automatic rifleman and a carrier to silence a machine-gun nest in his immediate front. The ammunition carrier was promptly killed, and Captain Skinker taking his ammunition continued on, firing the automatic rifle, until he met death himself, followed immediately by the automatic rifleman. Captain Skinker has been recommended for the Distinguished Service Medal, posthumous."

That same officer also wrote to Skinker's parents, "I looked upon his poor body lying where he fell in the road. His face bore the serene and peaceful expression of his waking hours."

When the commanding general reviewed the exact circumstances, he decided that the Distinguished Service Medal was not adequate. He determined that The Medal of Honor was more appropriate.

Colonel McMahon, who at one time commanded the regiment, wrote, "It is agreed that a man among men died a man's death, for America wonderful, quiet, heroic." Another man described him as, "in the day of battle calmly resolute and absolutely fearless."

Those in St. Louis who knew him shared the admiration that was expressed by his fellow soldiers. His funeral was held at Christ Church Cathedral and it was attended by over 1,200 people. Then a long procession wound its way to the Bellefontaine Cemetery where over 5,000 more people stood to honor him. His casket was draped with an American flag and carried by a caisson. The procession included two companies of infantry and a bugler along with nine men who were with him in the battle made the last call and fired the final salute over the hero's grave.

Smythe, James Anderson – Frontier Indian Campaigns

James Anderson Smythe was born in Quebec, Canada on May 28, 1849. Little is known about his life there but, when he was about twenty-one, he emigrated into the United States and enlisted in the Army. At that time he began using the name James Anderson. He served his entire military career with his middle name serving as his last. It's interesting to speculate as to why he did this.

He served in the 6th U.S. Cavalry and was assigned to frontier duty in northwest Texas. This was known as the 5th Military District and it was an unbelievably rough place to be. Its territory ranged from Brazos Santiago Harbor, (previously Port Matamoros), at the Mexican border, north to Louisiana. General Phil Sheridan was the first Military Governor but he was removed by President Jackson because of charges of harsh treatment of former Confederate soldiers serving in the unit. Even under the new Military Governors, several incidents were committed against African-American soldiers at Fort Brown in Brownsville.

The soldiers stationed in this area were routinely attacked by terrorists from Kansas known as Jayhawkers, by Indians, and by desperados from the U.S. and Mexico. Soldiers were often murdered by Jayhawkers and other outlaws seemingly just to get their weapons. The reports usually would just say, "Murdered by citizens unknown." When we add in the heat and the heavy dark blue uniforms, it was truly a rough tour of duty.

On October 5, 1870, the 6th Cavalry was fighting a running battle with Indians at the Little Wichita River. In some records it was noted as the "Skirmish at Bluff Creek." Very few details remain, even in official reports, about what happened that day. We might suppose that it was just another day of skirmishing with someone. But the actions of James Anderson stood out and he was awarded with the Medal of Honor. He Citation simply says:

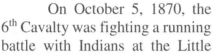

"Gallantry during the pursuit and fight with Indians."

James remained in the Army for ten more years and eventually rose to the rank of Second Lieutenant. He married Nellie Hanlon on November 14, 1880 and they moved to St. Louis. There he found employment as a stationery engineer. If this is correct, he must have specialized in some sort of paperwork. If the records are in error and he was a stationary engineer, then he worked with operating and maintaining machinery.

James' health began to fail him in 1917 and on May 31, 1918, he died of pneumonia. He is buried at St. Peter and Paul's Cemetery in St. Louis. He was joined in St. Peter and Paul's by his wife, Nellie, several weeks later.

Specker, Joe C. – World War II

Joe Specker was born January 10, 1921 in the nice little (population 1,800) farm town of Odessa, Missouri. Their high school teams are known as the Bulldogs and that seems a good name for the tough and tenacious people they have turned out. Those small town bulldogs include two Olympic Medalists in Gymnastics, Two professional mixed martial artists, a professional baseball pitcher and a recipient of our nation's

highest honor, the Medal of Honor. Oh yes, they also produced an undefeated State Champion football team in 2019.

Joe has been described as quiet, soft-spoken, and well-liked by those who knew him. But he hardly seemed to be a person you would expect to become a national hero. Linda Gillis, a reporter for _The Odessan_ newspaper is very knowledgeable about Joe Specker's life and she tells us that his favorite clothing would include a comfortable old pair of overalls. Specker loved malted milkshakes and pecan candy. He was chosen Captain of his high school baseball team and spent most of his free time playing baseball or going into town to see his fiancé, Mary Margaret Hok.

He joined the Army in September of 1942 and it was wartime so things happened fast. By January 7, 1944 he was already a veteran Sergeant serving with the 48th Engineer Combat Battalion. They were engaging German troops at Mount Porchia, Italy. Specker voluntarily went forward alone to destroy an enemy machine gun emplacement and was severely wounded. But he continued on leaving a trail of blood up the hill. His last message to the troops behind him was that he was "running out of Germans." Indeed, he was successful in routing the enemy force before he died. For his actions on this day, he was posthumously awarded the Medal of Honor.

His Medal of Honor citation reads:

"For conspicuous gallantry and intrepidity at risk of life, above and beyond the call of duty, in action involving actual conflict. On the night of 7 January 1944, Sgt. Specker, with his company, was advancing up the slope of Mount Porchio, Italy. He was sent forward on reconnaissance and on his return he reported to his company commander the fact that there was an enemy machinegun nest and several well-placed snipers directly in the path and awaiting the company. Sgt. Specker requested and was granted

permission to place 1 of his machineguns in a position near the enemy machinegun. Voluntarily and alone he made his way up the mountain with a machinegun and a box of ammunition."

"He was observed by the enemy as he walked along and was severely wounded by the deadly fire directed at him. Though so seriously wounded that he was unable to walk, he continued to drag himself over the jagged edges of rock and rough terrain until he reached the position at which he desired to set up his machinegun. He set up the gun so well and fired so accurately that the enemy machine-gun nest was silenced and the remainder of the snipers forced to retire, enabling his platoon to obtain their objective."

"Sgt. Specker was found dead at his gun. His personal bravery, self-sacrifice, and determination were an inspiration to his officers and fellow soldiers."

When people back home in Odessa learned that Joe Specker would be recognized with a Medal of Honor, the entire population was invited to attend the ceremony in the high school gymnasium. The invitation said, "Every citizen of Odessa and community should be present at this time. You will probably never be able to attend another such meeting."

Joe Specker was a nice young man, a hard-worker, and unimaginably brave. Joe Specker's life was too short but he will never be forgotten.

Stokes, Alonzo – Frontier Indian Campaigns

Alonzo Stokes was born in Middleburg, Ohio on July 10, 1836, the son of John and Mary Asher Stokes. He was almost twenty-five years old when the 6th Cavalry Regiment was formed on May 7, 1861. He joined that regiment and served throughout the Civil War earning the rank of First Sergeant.

Following that conflict, he stayed in the Army and was sent west to help settlers, miners, and others who were also going west from the war-torn states. In the summer of 1870, he was in the 5th Military District in Northwest Texas. We invite the reader to look back to the story of James Anderson Smythe to remember the wild situation in that area.

Sergeant Stokes was awarded the Medal of Honor for his bravery in action on July 12, 1870 at the Battle of the Little Wichita River. His Citation for the award says simply, "Gallantry in action." In that day's action he was one of 57 men from the 6th Cavalry pursuing of 250-strong group of Kiowa warriors led by Chief Kicking Bird. They pursued the Kiowas for five days, and finally met them on the Wichita River in Archer County, Texas. After a short initial fight, the cavalrymen found that they were outnumbered and outgunned.

231

They fought a fierce defensive battle that left three soldiers and fifteen Kiowas dead. After the Kiowas broke off the engagement in the early evening, the soldiers retreated, eventually making it back to Fort Richardson near Jacksboro, Texas.

Sergeant Stokes' Medal of Honor was presented to him at Fort Richardson on August 25, 1870. He was transferred back to Jefferson Barracks at St. Louis where he spent the remainder of his life.

On July 4, 1876, Stokes was trying to push a ram rod down the bore of cannon at Jefferson Barracks when it exploded killing him immediately. The 39-year-old First Sergeant was buried there in the National Cemetery at Jefferson Barracks.

Swearer, Benjamin – Civil War

Benjamin Swearer was born on May 18, 1825 in Baltimore. As a young man, he joined the Navy and was serving as a Seaman on the USS Pawnee (pictured below) when the War Between the States erupted. His duties were listed as "Captain of the Foretop." So his "battle station" was with the cannon nearest the foreword mast of the Sloop of War. This particular Sloop of War was powered by both steam and sail.

Early in the war, the Hatteras Inlet was a perfect place for Southern raiders to wait until commercial shipping came by. Then the raiders would dash out to seize the ships and their cargoes. It was a terrible headache for the Northern Navy and merchants. The Navy was determined to use their superior forces to take control of the harbor but it was guarded by several earthen forts.

On August 29, 1861 the Union Navy sent seven warships into the Inlet to land 880 Army and Navy personnel. They were tasked with overwhelming the earthen forts and clearing the way for the Navy's ships. Seaman Swearer took part in the attack on Fort Clark. His Medal of Honor Citations describes his actions on that occasion.

> *"Embarked in a surfboat from the U.S.S. Pawnee during action against Fort Clark, off Baltimore Inlet, August 29, 1861. Taking part in a mission to land troops and to remain inshore and provide protection, Swearer rendered gallant service throughout the action and had the honor of being the first man to raise the flag on the captured fort."*

We are fortunate to have a description of the event in the words of Seaman Swearer himself. This is his account of the events of that engagement:

"When the war began, I was an enlisted man on the Pawnee, United States sloop; I was gun-captain of No. 1 gun on my ship, which was lying in the Potomac, near Alexandria. One morning we got the order to land in this town. I went on shore, in charge of a crew; we were under command of Lieutenant Lowry. My men and I went into the city; I hoisted the American colors on the Beal and Everett post, at the corner of King and Queen Streets. Just while we were at this work, we heard of the murder of Colonel Ellsworth, who, while pulling down a Confederate standard at the Marshall House, had been shot dead by Mr. Jackson, the proprietor."

"We then proceeded to Michael s Point, down the river, and, in spite of the overwhelming fire from the rebel

batteries, we set fire to and burned the wharf. There was a tremendous cannonade from Mathias Point, and Captain Ward was killed by a shell."

"Our little vessels had to withdraw before the overwhelming fire. We were ordered to Norfolk, Va., from there back to Washington, and soon after to proceed to

Fairmount Point, Va. From here we went, under command of Flag Officer S. H. Stringham, to restore Federal authority over Hatteras Inlet and the adjacent waters of Chesapeake Bay, which was said to have become the resort of Confederate privateers. The squadron consisted of the frigates Minnesota and Wabash, the sloops Cumberland and Susquehanna, the steamers Pawnee, Harriet Lane and Fanny. The Fanny was a transport with 860 soldiers on board, under command of General Butler; we were to co-operate with them at Hatteras Inlet."

"There were two forts there, Fort Clark, near the outer liar, and Fort Hatteras, further on the inside. The day after leaving Norfolk, that is on the 27th of August, 1861, we anchored off Hatteras Inlet. The works were about half a mile off to the southwest, separated from us by a shallow bay, and they mounted together twenty-five guns, which we at that time, of course, did not know."

"In the evening the land troops were put ashore on the island, under cover of the guns of the squadron. Next morning, on the 25th, the fighting began. The first day we passed up and down before the forts, bombarding all the time, with the larger ships, while

235

the smaller ones accompanied the transport to a point
further north on the island to land the troops. I was
one of the landing party from the Pawnee, and shortly
after noon of the first day we got into Fort Clark. I
happened to be the first to hoist the Union flag in this
fort, for which deed I was granted the Naval Medal of
Honor. Towards noon the second day. the 29th, Fort
Hatteras showed the white flag. We took (515
Confederate prisoners, with 25 guns, 1,000 muskets
and a large supply of ordnance stores."

After the war, Swearer moved to Eastern Missouri and
settled in St. Louis County. He died on November 2, 1902 at
age seventy-seven and is buried at Saint Peter's Cemetery in
Normandy.

Now, here's something interesting to consider. You see, we
found an article in an 1855 newspaper describing a trial in St.
Louis at that time. In short, on September 8, 1855, in St. Louis
Criminal Court, the trial of a man named Benjamin Swearer was
concluded and the jury rendered a guilty verdict of Murder in
the Third Degree. In today's terms, that would be comparable
to involuntary manslaughter. The victim was a woman named
Vera Wadsworth. The defendant was sentenced to three years
in the state Penitentiary in Jefferson City.

So, is it possible that Swearer's time in the Navy followed
a prison term in Jefferson City? Did he have problems finding
a good job after prison? Did he go back to the place of his birth
and enlist in the Navy? Returning to Missouri after the war with
a Medal of Honor would certainly do a lot to help improve his
opportunities for a good life. What do you think?

An Impression of Frontier Cavalrymen

Before meeting our next hero, the reader can profit from the impressions of a man who actually did meet the men in the following story. Theo. F. Rodenbough compiled a collection of stories centered around men who earned the Medal of Honor in the early days. He left a marvelous description of the soldiers just prior to their journey in pursuit of the Tonto Apaches. Though he thought they looked more like bandits than soldiers, he was still impressed. His description gives a very different picture than the images we get from motion pictures and television.

> *"Let us inspect these frontier soldiers. We look in vain, with our civilized eyes, for the " pomp and circumstance " which one associates with a "regular" in the East at Washington or New York. Where are the plumes and pipe-clay? where the dazzling brasses and the faultless cut of the company tailor? A search in the men's lockers would doubtless reveal them, snugly packed away for the next garrison duty. But here another garb, a combination of experience and the old-clothes bag, is the correct thing."*

> *"We may perhaps except the detachment commander.(Lieutenant Charles King) His clothes are not shabby; and he can't help being neat, even when on*

a " scout." *From the top of his low-crowned, feather-weight, drab, felt hat to the dark-blue flannel shirt, fastened at the neck with a knotted silk handkerchief, and the small soft gauntlet which he twirls restlessly in one hand, the artist as well as the campaigner stands out; he of all the party wears closely-fitting cavalry breeches, boots, spurs, and a cartridge-belt well filled; an " officer s rifle " completes a picturesque and useful outfit.*

"Standing by his horse, a little apart from the men, is an admirable specimen of the Irish-American soldier. Of medium stature, very powerfully built, with a frank, bronzed face, bright blue eyes and close-cut auburn hair and mustache (marked in the descriptive list as "sandy "), Sergeant Bernard Taylor of the Fifth Horse would at a glance be picked out as one of the best men in the party. His costume, although hardly as natty as that of his superior, is not less adapted to the nature of the service.

"A gray felt sombrero, with upturned brim, is clapped well down on his head, with a gentle inclination over the right eyebrow ; a faded lead-colored flannel shirt, open at the neck, gives a glimpse of a red undershirt ; a plains-man s home-made cartridge-belt, bristling with metallic ammunition, encircles his waist, with a revolver on one side, balanced on the other by a keen-bladed hunting-knife ; buckskin breeches, and well-greased cowhide boots, with huge rowelled Mexican spurs, make up the Sergeant's equipment.

"The short-limbed, compactly-built, California horse, standing quietly at his elbow, looks fit for any emergency, and has more than once shown a clean pair of heels to the enemy, when discretion on his rider's part has been the better part of valor; the McClellan saddle, stripped of every ounce of unnecessary leather, and

planted well forward on the neatly folded blanket, the snug sack of barley, like a small section of stove-pipe resting behind the cantle of the saddle, the extra girth, all these are signs that mean business.

"The rest are more or less similarly accoutred. Hardly a forage cap, not a sabre, nor a letter or number to tell to what particular regiment of Uncle Sam's retainers these bandit-like horsemen belong."

Taylor, Bernard – Indian Wars

Bernard Taylor was born in St. Louis but he didn't stay there. He really got around! When he was old enough, he left St. Louis and went first to the East Coast. While there (in Washington, D.C.) he signed on as a Private in the US 5th Cavalry and, with them, he went west. He traveled and served through the plains and mountain territories. By the time he was thirty years old, he had proven himself in the Apache Wars and moved up to the rank of Sergeant. Author, Theo. F. Rodenbough said that, "Bernard Taylor, was called 'Barney' by the troopers when off duty, but respectfully addressed 'Sergeant' at all other times. Both King and Eaton knew him well. He had been in many a scout and skirmish with the regiment, and was hailed as a daring, resolute, intelligent man, and a non-commissioned officer of high merit."

He was known to be an expert horseman, a quick and accurate shot, a gallant and enthusiastic trooper, and he loved the rough mountain scouting. The city boy turned frontier soldier was still in Arizona on November 1, 1874. That morning Sergeant Taylor set out with a detachment led by Lieutenant Charles King. They were in search of Apaches – and they found them. From Sunset Pass, near the Little Colorado River, they began to climb a mesa to reach a higher point for reconnaissance of the surrounding area. Then, a band of Tonto Apaches opened fire from above. Lieutenant King was hit in his head and eye. Soon another bullet shattered his arm. Taylor came to King's aid and, under heavy fire all the while, carried the half-conscious young officer half a mile back to safety. King knew how perilous their situation was and he told Sergeant Taylor to leave him. But Taylor continued and completed his daring rescue. The Lieutenant's wounds led to his discharge from the Army and he became a popular author writing about history and fiction. He also took the time to write Washington and nominate Sergeant Taylor for the Medal of

Honor sighting his selfless action and conspicuous bravery.

On April 12, 1875 Bernard Taylor was thirty-one years old and he received the Medal of Honor. The Campaign was in its last days and he, like the other men, were looking forward to returning home for a while. But Taylor was ill with lung congestion and, two days after receiving his medal, he died. His body was taken to San Francisco and buried in a place of honor at the National Cemetery.

This illustration by military artist, Rufus Fairchild Zogbaum shows Sergeant Taylor rescuing First Lieutenant Charles King at Sunset Pass. It was used in Theo F. Rodenbough's book, Uncle Sam's Medal of Honor (1886).

Toohey, Thomas P. – Civil War

Thomas Toohey was born on New Year's Day, 1835. His family lived in New York City at that time. His parents, Peter and Sarah (Jennings) Toohey were natives of Ireland. Peter hailed from County Mayo and Sarah from County Galway. They married in 1830 and came to America soon after. Peter had been a seafarer but in America, and with a family, he settled down to a job with the local Gas Light Company. He stayed there and with that job for the rest of his life.

Thomas, on the other hand, seemed to have inherited his parents' love to move on and he went west. In 1855 he accepted a job with the Illinois Central Railroad. He stayed with that railroad until the war began between North and South. He left the train in Milwaukee and joined the 24th Wisconsin Infantry. That was on August 6, 1862 so he was twenty-seven years old. Having been a member of the National Guard in New York, he was made a Sergeant because of his previous experience.

He was wounded at the Battle of Franklin (Tennessee), and fought at Perryville, Stone River, Chickamauga, Missionary Ridge, Dundridge, Rocky Face Ridge, Calhoun, Dallas, Kenesaw Mountain, Peach Tree Creek, Jonesboro, and Nashville.

At the Battle of Franklin, he was recognized for his courage and rewarded with the Medal of Honor. His Citation tells us:

"For gallantry in action on 30 November 1864, while serving with Company F, 24th Wisconsin Infantry, in action at Franklin, Tennessee. Sergeant Toohey voluntarily assisting in working guns of battery near right of the regiment after nearly every man had left them, the fire of the enemy being hotter at this than at any other point on the line."

He served throughout the remainder of the war and was discharged on June 10, 1865. He went back temporarily to his old job in Milwaukee but then he decided to move further west. He followed an opportunity to take a position as an engineer on the supply train as the Missouri, Kansas, & Texas (KATY) Railroad was being built. By 1869, he was settled in Kansas City. On Thanksgiving Day, 1877, he married Laura J. Barnes and they made their home at 806 West 14th Street in Kansas City. (That property is now the lawn of the Clarence M. Kelley F.B.I. Campus.) They had two sons, Walter and Thomas, Jr. That younger Thomas followed in his father's footsteps and became a well-known engineer with the St. Louis – San Francisco Railroad. (the Frisco)

On April 8, 1878, Kanas City's Union Depot opened in what is called the West Bottoms. Critics called the Depot the "Jackson County Insane Asylum" because it was such a crazy idea. Everyone knew it was too extremely large. Of course the city outgrew the Union Depot and had to replace it with the magnificent Union Station. But back in 1878, Tom Toohey claimed the honor of being the engineer on the first train to leave the Union Depot.

Thomas invested his earnings wisely and in 1893 (age 58) he retired to manage his properties in Kansas City. He was well-known and well-liked in Kansas City and some Republicans hoped he might run for office but he never did. One of his retirement activities was to organize civic and veterans' groups into action keeping the cemeteries maintained. This was especially important at the graves of veterans on what they used to call "Decoration Day." Now of course, we call it Memorial Day.

Thomas Toohey was eighty-three when his life journey ended on November 19, 1918. He is buried in Mount Washington Cemetery, Garden of Valor Section, Independence, Missouri. Laura joined him there in 1932.

Author's Note:

It is hoped that many will read the "thumbnail biographies" presented in this book and be inspired to learn more about the various men who are portrayed. If you are researching Thomas Toohey, it is important to recognize that during the time when Thomas lived in Kansas City there was another Thomas Toohey who was a notorious criminal and who was very active in the K. C. Area. The two men are not related in any way.

Townsend, Julius Curtis – Siege of Veracruz

Julius Curtis Townsend was born February 22, 1881 in Athens, Missouri. That's up in Clark County and the Northeastern corner of the state. He was one of six children born to James and Harriet (Curtis) Townsend. Julius was named for his mother's father, Julius C. Curtis. His father's parents had come to Clark County in 1830.

Julius' father was James W. Townsend, the largest grain dealer in the area. In 1878 he married Miss Hattie Curtis, also from Athens. In 1882 he ran for office and was elected Circuit Court Clerk. He spent a good deal of his time then in the County Seat at Kahoka. Julius ran the family business during the four years that James was in office. We mention all of this to show that Julius' family was hard-working, prosperous and well-respected merchants and an important part of the agricultural community. The fact that he was accepted into the Naval Academy tells us that he was a good student and a responsible young man.

After completing high school, he entered the Naval Academy at Annapolis. he graduated from the United States Naval Academy in 1902 and was commissioned an Ensign in 1904. He was Lieutenant Townsend on April 21, 1914 when the US was locked in turmoil at Veracruz in Mexico.

One year earlier Victoria Huerta had taken control of Mexico in a bloody coup and the relationship between Huerta and the United States was very poor. Then nine American sailors were arrested in the Mexican city of Veracruz and the American Naval Commander demanded their release, an apology from Mexico, and a twenty-one gun salute. The sailors were released, an apology was provided, but the symbolic salute was not provided.

At this time it was also learned that a shipload of weapons was scheduled to arrive on a German ship at the Port of Veracruz. President Wilson decided not to let that happen so he ordered the Navy to seize the port. Three Navy rifle companies, known as Bluejackets, were sent to capture the post office, the telegraph offices, and the Customs House. Marines were dispatched to seize the Railroad Terminal, the yards, and the roundhouse. They were also to take the Electric Power Plant and the Cable Office. By 1:30 the ship loaded with weapons and ammunition was intercepted and detained. 587 Marines and Navy personnel were involved on that first day. Four were killed and twenty wounded.

The next morning it was decided that the Americans would not be successful unless they took control of the entire city. More than 3000 sailors and marines were offloaded from the fleet. The Marines were not accustomed to street fighting but they adapted. The Bluejackets didn't adapt as well. One Captain even took his men to attack the Naval Academy while they were dressed in their best and in parade ground formation. They were easy targets. The Captain then called for support and the fleet opened up with big guns on the Academy and ended all resistance. For the first time in history, naval aviators flew over the battle and provided intelligence for the officers below. Also, for the first time in American military history, our aviators were the target of groundfire. By the end of that second day, 6,000 American personnel were ashore.

Fifty-six Medals of Honor were awarded for that two-day campaign. That's about half the number for all of World War I. One Marine, Major Smedley Butler, received one of the medals and complained bitterly about it. He tried to return it and called it an, "unutterable foul perversion of Our Country's greatest gift." He claimed that he had done nothing heroic. The Navy told him to keep it and to wear it.

It's hard to know exactly what Lieutenant Townsend did on April 22 to earn his medal. His Citation only tells us:

> *"For distinguished conduct in battle, engagement of Vera Cruz, 22 April 1914. Lt. Townsend was eminent and conspicuous in command of his battalion. He exhibited courage and skill in leading his men through the action of the 22d and in the final occupation of the city."*

Julius Townsend remained in the Navy and rose through the ranks. In 1926 Captain Townsend was in command of the USS Galveston (Cruiser) during a time of great civil unrest in the Central American and Caribbean countries. On August 27, 1926 she arrived at Bluefields, Nicaragua and landed a force of 195 men following a request of the American Consul to protect American interests during a revolutionary uprising. At this time, Captain Townsend again distinguished himself and was awarded the Navy Cross.

Remaining in the Navy, he served as Commander of our Naval Aviation Base, in County Cork, Ireland during World War I. He was in command of the Cruisers Battle Forces in 1936.

He retired as a Rear Admiral in the spring of 1939 but he died on December 28 of that year at age 58. He is buried at the Arlington National Cemetery.

Our Thanks:

We thankfully acknowledge the contributions of Brenda Brown and the H.E. Sever Memorial Library in Kahoka, MO.

Tracy, John –
Frontier
Indian Campaigns

It seems that Henry George Nabers got on the ship and John Tracy got off. I'll explain. On December 28, 1848 Henry G. Nabers was born in Dublin, Ireland. Then, while still a young man, he left for America. When he departed from his ship, he gave his name as John Tracy. He later said that, when he was eighteen, he ran away from home and changed names so his parents wouldn't be able to find him. To make matters more confusing for us, he sometimes switched back-and-forth between the two names.

At any rate he was in the United States in 1869 and enlisted in the Army as a Private. He was sent to the West to serve in the 8th U.S. Cavalry during the Apache Wars. Cochise and his followers were in the Chiricahua Mountains of Arizona and refusing to be subdued by the Army. This action later became known as the "Campaign of the Rocky Mesa."

The 8ᵗʰ U.S. Cavalry on Parade

On October 5, 1869, he was with a small cavalry detachment from Fort Bowie that was in pursuit of an Apache raiding party. This particular raiding party had massacred those aboard a stage coach headed for Tucson. Then they attacked a group of cowboys in the Sulphur Springs Valley.

The cavalry unit finally caught up to the Apaches at Cochise's stronghold above Rucker Canyon. A major battle took place on that October 20, 1869. The records aren't specific about what Private Tracy did that day but he was presented with the Medal of Honor for his actions. The Medal of Honor Citation says simply:

"Bravery in action with Indians."

Twenty-five years later, John told a reporter, "For my conduct in this battle, I received a medal from the Government but that medal has since been lost."

On another mission, John was in charge of nine men who were to drive about 50 cattle to their fort but were attacked by Natives. John was shot through the foot with an arrow and every other man received a wound of some kind. In the end only three made it back to the fort and John was the only one who didn't lose an arm or leg.

John married Mary Marthaler November 27, 1873 and they chose St. Louis as their home. They were living in St. Louis before 1883 and all of their children were born there. It seems that he went back to using his original name, Henry George Nabers, at about this time and he lived with Mary at 1318 North 15th Street.

John Tracy died on May 29, 1918 at age 69 and was interred at the Calvary Cemetery and Mausoleum in St. Louis, Missouri. He was buried in an unmarked grave and remained that way for nearly a century. Finally, a campaign, headed by Connie Nisinger in the spring of 2003, resulted in an official Medal of Honor headstone being placed at his grave site. Mary and several of their children also rest in Calvary Cemetery.

Trogden,
Howell Gilliam –
Civil War

Look for the story of Howell Gilliam Trogden in the section on the Missouri Men of Forlorn Hope on page 68.

Wherry, William Mackey – Civil War

William M. Wherry, usually called "Macky" by his friends, was born in St. Louis on September 13, 1836, the grandson of an Irish immigrant who was very successful in his New World business dealings. This grandfather, Mackay Wherry, had settled in St. Louis before the Louisiana Purchase (1798) and was the settlement's first Register (Town Clerk). This Irish grandfather was also credited with organizing St. Louis' first police force.

Macky attended the University of Missouri in Columbia and then returned to St. Louis as a merchant. When the Civil War began, he enlisted as a 1st Lieutenant in the 3rd Reserve, Missouri Infantry. He served on General Lyon's staff during the Battle of Wilson's Creek on August 10, 1861. At Wilson's Creek, Lyon became the first Northern General to die during the war. But Wherry received the Medal of Honor for "Conspicuous coolness and heroism in rallying troops that were recoiling under heavy fire."

Lieutenant S. O. Fish was at Wilson's Creek and he described Wherry's actions that day:

"About 9 o'clock the Company occupied a part of the general line and was especially in support of a section of Totten's battery. We had suffered seriously in the fierce contest which had preceded and about this hour were heavily assailed by fresh troops and a most destructive fire, under which the men recoiled and the Company broke and abandoned the line. While I was engaged in the utmost endeavor to rally the men, and while my efforts seemed almost hopeless, Lieut. Wm. M. Wherry. . .seeing my dilemma and quickly realizing the danger of losing the guns of the battery, came to my assistance. Lieut. Wherry displayed unusual coolness and heroism. He aided me in stopping the men and infused renewed confidence among them, got them back into the line and remained with me until the guns and position were safe."

That certainly gives us a better idea of what happened to earn the Medal for Lieutenant Wherry, doesn't it?

In 1861, he was promoted to first lieutenant in the Regular Army. He served in staff positions for various officers for the remainder of the war and rose to the rank of Major. On March 13, 1865, he was brevetted to Brigadier General of Volunteers. His promotion was said to be for gallant and meritorious services. He was chosen to carry the surrender papers from General Johnston's army to Washington, in 1865.

When the war ended, Wherry remained in the Regular Army and served for a short time as General John Schofield's military secretary. During the Spanish-American War, he was promoted to Colonel in the Regular Army and to Brigadier General of Volunteers. He also went west to serve in the Frontier Indian Wars in Montana.

Gen. Wherry went to Europe with Gen. Schofield in 1865. They were on a special mission warning Europeans (especially the French) about their intervention in Mexico. In 1874, King Kamehameha from Hawaii was touring the United States and General Wherry was chosen to accompany the King on his tour. He retired in 1899 with the rank of brigadier general.

Back in June of 1868, Captain Wherry had wed Alice Wilms of Baltimore. By 1870, they had moved to Macky's home in Missouri and their first child was born. They had six more children over the next several years. After retiring, he and Alice took a cruise around the world.

Two of Macky's daughters had moved to Cincinnati and, late in life, he purchased a home to be near them and his grandchildren. On November 3, 1918, he was in Cincinnati and died while there. He was brought back to his hometown and is buried in Bellefontaine Cemetery, St. Louis.

Wilson, Richard G. — Korean War

Born August 19, 1931, Richard started life in Marion, Illinois. But when he was eight, his family moved the few miles to Cape Girardeau. There he grew up with his three brothers and three sisters. He attended May Greene Elementary School and Central High School. He was a tough kid and played right guard on the high school football team. He was also a respected amateur boxer.

But, as with many young men at that time, he left high school and joined the Army. That was on his seventeenth birthday and he was just one year short of graduation. He took his Basic Training at fort Knox, Kentucky and then went to Fort Sam Houston in Texas for combat medic training. Completing that, he went to Airborne School at Fort Benning, Georgia. His graduation from Airborne was in May, 1949.

His first duty station was at Fort Campbell, Kentucky with the 11th Airborne Division. On the 29th of August, 1950, Richard married his high school sweetheart, Yvonna Fowler.

He was deployed soon after that to Korea with the 187th Airborne Infantry Regiment.

On the 21st of October, 1950 Pfc. Wilson was on a reconnaissance mission near Opa-ri and serving as a combat medic when his company was ambushed by a numerically superior force. There were many casualties and many of those men were down in places they could not be reached safely, but this nineteen-year-old Private went to their aid anyway.

He exposed himself to extreme hostile fire in order to treat the many wounded. Then, when the company began to pull back, he exposed himself again as he helped to evacuate the wounded. When he thought the withdrawal was complete, he learned that one soldier had been left behind and was trying to crawl to safety.

Richard, against the advice of others, went to the aid of the wounded man. He was not seen again until two days later when his body was found lying next to the man he had gone to help. It was for these actions in what has come to be called the Battle of Yongju, that Richard Wilson was rewarded with the Medal of Honor.

The teenager from Cape Girardeau is remembered today in the following places:

- ✪ A memorial to Wilson in Cape County Park
- ✪ The Richard G. Wilson Consolidated Troop Medical Clinic in Fort Leonard Wood, MO
- ✪ The Richard G. Wilson Memorial Gymnasium in the Kanoka Barracks at Osaka, Japan
- ✪ The Richard G. Wilson U.S. Army Reserve Center in Carbondale, Illinois
- ✪ The Richard G. Wilson Elementary School in Fort Benning, Georgia
- ✪ The Richard G. Wilson postal distribution center in Cape Girardeau, Missouri
- ✪ The PFC Richard G. Wilson Training Barracks at Fort Sam Houston, Texas
- ✪ The Wilson Theater in Fort Campbell, Kentucky

Show Me More Heroes

There have been many Missourians who might have been recognized with a Medal of Honor but were not. This writer suggests four that deserve consideration for that great honor. Read on and see if you agree. These short sketches are from the book *Missouri's Forgotten Heroes*.

England, John – World War II

If you ever visit England City Park in Caruthersville, you might be amazed to see a jet plane in the park along with some information about a true American hero. By the time John England got his pilot's wings, (1943) World War II was half over. But he still managed to become an "Ace" in just the short time he had for wartime. During those two years he shot down nineteen German planes!

He was awarded the Silver Star Citation a year later and this is how the Citation read:

"For gallantry in action while participating in a fighter sweep over Germany, 27 November 1944. Sighting a formation of approximately fifty (50) hostile fighters, Captain England unhesitatingly led his Flight to the attack. By skillful maneuvering, he gained the initial advantage of surprise and was successful in destroying two (2) FW-190's. Having become separated from the rest of his Flight, he never-the-less exhibited utter disregard for personal danger by engaging alone another large force of enemy aircraft. Although only three (3) of his guns were now operational, he pressed home his attack with such forceful determination that he was able to shoot down two (2) more enemy planes before withdrawing. Captain England's gallantry and zealous desire to destroy the enemy at all costs served as an inspiration to all who participated in the action."

Before war's end, Colonel England had participated in 108 missions for the Army Air Corps. Then the Air Corps became the Air Force and England continued in that organization until his early death in 1954. Even his death was heroic.

He was on temporary duty while serving as Commander of the 399th Fighter-Bomber Squadron in France. While approaching his air base for landing, his F-86 engine failed. The prudent thing to do would be to eject and parachute to safety. However, doing that would most likely cause the jet to fall into the barracks complex below. So Col. England stayed aboard his falling aircraft and manually steered it away from the barracks. He knowingly sacrificed his own life to avoid harming anyone in those barracks.

Today, England Air Force Base in Alexandria, Louisiana is named to honor Col. England. But he has always remained the biggest hero for those in his home town of Caruthersville.

Pruitt,
Wendall Oliver –
World War II

Wendell Oliver Pruitt was born (June 20, 1920) and grew up in St. Louis as the youngest of ten children. He graduated from Sumner High School in that city then went on to attend the Stowe Teachers College (Now Harris-Stowe State U). But he soon left that school for Lincoln University in Jefferson City. It was there that he learned to fly and earned his pilot's license at the Jefferson City Airport. It was, in fact, the civil aviation program that drew him to Lincoln U.

Upon graduation in 1941 he enrolled at Tuskegee Institute and the US Army Flying School. By 1942 he was flying fighter planes and was flying P-47 Thunderbolts in the Mediterranean Theater.

There Pruitt teamed up with Lt. Col. Lee Archer in the 332nd Fighter Group. If pressed to name just one, the men of the 322nd would tell you that Wendell Pruitt was the best pilot in the entire group but his wingman, Archer, was close. These two outstanding pilots came to be known as "The Gruesome Twosome." The Gruesome Twosome was featured in a History Channel presentation entitled, "Dogfights: Tuskegee Airmen."

Pruitt flew seventy combat missions and is credited with shooting down three enemy planes. In June of 1944 he and his wingman made direct hits on a German destroyer causing it to sink at Trieste. He also destroyed seventy German aircraft on the ground. Toward the end of the war the 332nd was flying the new P-51 Mustangs. He earned the Distinguished Flying Cross with six Oak Leaf Clusters.

You may have seen the movie "Red Tails" that features the exploits of the famous 322nd and their fighter planes with the distinctive painted tails. In the movie, the character of Joe "Lightening" Little was based on Pruitt and his amazing flying abilities.

In the closing days of the war, Captain Pruitt was sent back to the United States so he could teach other pilots at Tuskegee. It was there that he died in April 1945 when a student crashed his plane and killed Pruitt.

St. Louis city fathers named a housing project for him and also the Pruitt Military Academy. Even if you have seen the movie, did you know that this hero was one of ours? Well now we do!

Rieger, James –
World War I

A common occurrence in the 1800s was for a couple to move to the Heartland of America looking for opportunity and to flee the domestic warfare in Germany. Gottfried and Rose Rieger immigrated first to Illinois and then settled in Adair County, Missouri. Gottfried was a farmer and a cooper (barrel maker). He worked hard and prospered. They had two sons, Christopher and James.

James was educated in Adair County's rural schools and then went to the Normal School in Kirksville. (Now known as Truman State University.) He worked as a public school teacher and eventually he went to Law School at the University of Missouri. Upon graduation he returned to Kirksville and established his law practice. He served as the Prosecuting Attorney, School Board President, and much more.

Back at Mizzou, Rieger had been active in the Cadet Corps and then joined the Missouri Militia. In 1916, the now Major James Rieger joined with fellow-Missourian General John J. Pershing and pursued the bandit, Pancho Villa, into Mexico. Then came the U.S. entry into World War I.

The Missouri Militia was mustered into federal service and sent to France. His unit, the 35th Infantry Division was held in reserve for some time and then sent into the Argonne Offensive. Rieger led his men in an attack on the Hindenburg Line, then regrouped and attacked again, this time crossing the Aire River through heavy fire from enemy artillery and machine guns. Rieger's battalion captured the key village of Exermont and the German defenses were broken. They began to fall back with the Allies in pursuit.

The French and American newspapers called Rieger "The Hero of the Argonne." For his leadership and heroism, Rieger was promoted to Lieutenant Colonel and awarded the Distinguished Service Cross. The French awarded him the Croix de Guere for valor. He also received the Purple Heart for his wounds as well as four other medals for meritorious service.

I would also like to point out that his citation for meritorious service tells that he did not sit back and command the men to do the work. He led from the front of the unit and endured everything he asked his men to do. The *Evening Missourian* newspaper in Columbia interviewed two mustered out soldiers who said:

"We had a Major from Kirksville. His name was James E. Rieger. He was the major of the second battalion. He would do his best for us and there wasn't one of us that wouldn't go to Hell for him." The other man chimed in, *"He surely ought to be made Governor of Missouri."*

But Rieger was not interested in politics. He was very happy to settle back into the life of a small town Midwestern lawyer. He gave the nation two sons who also distinguished themselves in their military careers. In addition to their jobs in Kirksville, Nathaniel and Wray Rieger achieved the ranks of Colonel and General and gave service from Burma to Alaska, to Europe. Both distinguished themselves and earned many honors. Nathaniel, a lawyer like his father, served as a JAG officer and was named Commandant of the Judge Advocate General's School as well as being the Judge Advocate General for Europe.

Trivia:

In reporting to you about the personality and leadership style of James Rieger, I could not avoid thinking of some other Missouri military leaders who would lead from the front and were known for empathizing with the common soldier. In the War Between the States, the foot soldiers called General Sterling Price, "Old Pap." It's no wonder that a leader who is also a fatherly figure could be elected Governor. John J. Pershing, from Laclede, Missouri was known as "Black Jack" Pershing because of his experience in leading the black soldiers as well as teaching in a black school earlier. He was famous for his compassion.

The most outstanding in this category may have been General Omar Bradley from the Second World War. This Clark, Missouri native was called "The G.I.'s General" by the troops on the ground. He was famous for taking care of the men in his command. His compassion did not hinder him but helped him rise to the rank of a Five Star General. There have been only five men to ever attain that rank and Pershing and Bradley represent Missouri well.

Schrier, Harold George – World War II

Harold Schrier was born in little Corder, Missouri back in 1916. He grew up and went to school in Lexington, there in Lafayette County. Only a handful of people will recognize his name but every American knows what he did. In fact, his actions have been portrayed in countless ways and serve as an emblem for the American spirit and for the courage of the American military.

When he was twenty years old, he enlisted in the Marine Corps. One of his first duties was as an Embassy guard in Beijing. He also served in Tientsin and Shanghai then was sent back to San Diego to serve as a drill instructor. When the U.S. was drawn into World War II, Schrier was promoted to platoon sergeant and was sent to Midway Island as part of a Raider Battalion.

He participated in the Battle of Guadalcanal and in his battalion's "Long Patrol" behind enemy lines during November and December of 1942. During this "patrol" he distinguished himself by leading a part of his company to safety after an officer's error led them into a hostile situation. Soon after this, he was promoted to 2nd Lieutenant.

His next duties were startling and amazing. As the US forces carried out their "island hopping" strategy across the Pacific, many amphibious landings were carried out by the Marines. But before those landings, Lt. Schrier and his Raiders were charged with observing and doing reconnaissance on those targeted islands. Remember – these missions were done before the assault landings by the other Marines.

For his bravery in the face of danger on the island of Bangunu, Schrier was awarded the Legion of Merit. He was then assigned to duties at Bougainville and a return to the U.S. to become an infantry instructor at Camp Pendleton. His next assignment was as the Executive Officer of his company in the 5th Marine Division. He reported to Hawaii for additional training in preparation for the gruesome assault on the island of Iwo Jima. There were many Marines from Missouri involved in that battle. More than eighty of them were from St. Louis alone!

On February 23, 1945 Lt. Schrier volunteered to lead a forty-man combat patrol to the top of Mount Suribachi. They reached the top at approximately 10:30 that morning and planted a small flag to signal that the peak was now in American control. It was the first time that an American flag had ever flown over territory in the inner defenses of the Empire of Japan. Schrier himself, along with Sgt. Earnest Thomas and Sgt. Henry Hansen actually raised the flag. Volunteering for that action earned Schrier the Navy Cross.

Later that same day, someone decided that the flag was not large enough so they sent Schrier back up the mountain in charge of a detail whose duty was to raise a larger flag on a bigger pole. Joe Rosenthal of the Associated Press snapped a picture of that event and that is the one which has become immortalized in statuary and in print. It's interesting that Schrier did climb that mountain one more time. This time it was with John Wayne and others as they filmed the movie, *"Sands of Iwo Jima."*

Schrier was awarded the Silver Star Medal and continued to serve for the duration of the war. He was called to serve again in Korea and did so at the Battle of Pusan Perimeter. He earned a Bronze Star for his gallantry in that battle. While serving as a Company Commander, he was shot in the neck at a night fight in North Korea and was evacuated to Japan where he recovered. He continued to serve with honor until 1957 when he retired. By that time, he had risen from the position of a raw enlisted recruit to the rank of Lieutenant Colonel.

Epilogue

We should be aware of something unique in the Show-Me State. Jefferson Barracks was founded way back in 1826 and served as the Headquarters for all of our western military units. Some have said that it was the Pentagon of the West. Stephen W. Kearny was one of the first Commandants. Over 220 Civil War generals served at Jefferson Barracks during their military careers, such as Robert E. Lee, Ulysses S. Grant, Winfield Hancock, James Longstreet, and even Confederate President Jefferson Davis and American Presidents, Zachary Taylor and Dwight D. Eisenhower.

So, a lot of military heroes have connections to Missouri through that one post. In addition, many military men and women from all over the nation have been buried in the beautiful cemetery. Anyone living in Missouri should probably make plans for a visit to Jefferson Barracks Park and Museum. And, while you're there, look for the many Medal of Honor recipients interred.

In reading about the resolute men in this book, did you notice where they came from? They served this country from all over the world. More than half of America's Medal of Honor recipients are Irish-Americans and we saw that many of those Missourians shared a German heritage.

You may have noticed also that some were wealthy and held university degrees while some were impoverished and illiterate. Some came from our cities and many came from small towns and farms. The intrepid spirit can grow in many kinds of soil.

Some had been rejected when they first tried to enlist. But they didn't accept rejection. Those who survived carried their positive attitudes forward into their personal lives following the war and it served them well.

In collecting the biographical information for *Extreme Valor*, this writer was amazed at all of the teenagers he found in the military on both sides of the War Between the States. O. P. Howe and his little brother, Lyston, were good examples of that. But the youngest **Missourian to serve in the Civil War was** Charles Knecht. He was only 7 years, 10 ½ months old when he enrolled on Sept. 15, 1861. Knecht served for just under four months as a drummer with the Benton Cadets, a Union infantry unit formed in St. Louis. Although not activated, young Charles attempted to enlist again in September 1864, this time as a private in Co. F of the 40th MO Infantry.

Many left the military service to start businesses. Entrepreneurs will understand that starting a business takes courage, daring, sacrifice, and commitment so it should be no surprise to us that these men might become successful businessmen. Many bought land, farm implements, and livestock to establish farms. Others started photo studios, harness shops, restaurants, or mills. Others became trunk manufacturers, boot makers, and other self-employed craftsmen. At least two were inventors. Several invested their time and money to pursue education and join the professions. These men weren't the kind to sit back and wait for life to happen. They made things happen. We will always be indebted to them for their gallantry on the battlefield but we should also remember what people like these contribute to peacetime America.

We must never forget those who didn't have the opportunity to come home and make a fresh start. We owe them the most of all. For those who came home with "shell shock" or "PTSD" we owe them understanding and support. For all Medal of Honor recipients, <u>we owe them</u>!

When we think of all that the returning veterans accomplished in their business life and all of the fine families they left for Missouri and America, we have to wonder what might have become of those men who didn't return. What might they have accomplished and what might they have created and left for us?

When all is said, and done, and written about the men in this book, I thank God for these inspirational men of extreme valor!

Acknowledgements

We wish to acknowledge the following individuals and institutions who have generously contributed their information and knowledge. Without them, this book could not have been completed.

Katherine Owens, Curator of Collections, for Missouri's State Parks.

Peggy Buhr, Museum Director, at the Bates County Historical Society

Jennifer Said, Descendant of Henry Frizzell

Wayne and Marilyn Schuessler, Directors, at the historic St. Trinity Cemetery, Lemay

Linda Thompson of the *South Cass Tribune*

Harrisonville's local historian, Jackie Roberts.

Laura Sue Daniels and the folks at the Jewett-Norris Library in Trenton

B. J. Chadduck of the Franklin County (Missouri) Historical Society

Traci Bohannon and the Wright County Historical Society

Joe Sonderman, Missouri Historian

Mike Bender, Missouri Historian

Gail Shoush & the Civil War Soldiers Project of the Macon Co. Historical Society

Brenda Brown and the H.E. Sever Memorial Library in Kahoka

Gary Rustige, Military Consultant